The Lord
LOOKETH ON THE HEART

The Lord
LOOKETH ON THE HEART

MAX AND BETTE
MOLGARD

Bookcraft
Salt Lake City, Utah

Contents

If we could look into each other's hearts and understand the unique challenges each of us face, I think we would treat each other much more gently, with more love, patience, tolerance, and care.

—*Marvin J. Ashton*

1
Secrets of the Heart

HIDDEN IN THE CHEST OF OUR mortal bodies is a heart. This unseen organ of the body controls the physical well-being of our body by pumping nourishing red blood to every living cell. When the heart is strong, it does an efficient job and bathes every part of the body with its gift of oxygen. There are, however, many diseases and malfunctions of the heart that cause a lack of oxygen to the brain and other body parts. This lack of oxygen can cause many abnormal body functions that result in sickness and sometimes death. Because of its critical function, we could call the heart the life of the body.

Hidden in our soul is a spiritual heart. This unseen heart controls the spiritual well-being of our spirit. When this heart is strong, it does an efficient job of bathing every part of the spirit with its spiritual gifts. A healthy spiritual heart radiates its gifts and blesses countless other lives as it touches and warms.

There are, however, many diseases and malfunctions of this spiritual heart that can result in spiritual sickness and malfunction. They are the result of the hard knocks of life: a neglectful home, an abusive husband, a verbal slap in the face—the list goes on and on. With each negative nudge or tackle of life comes a new scar on the spiritual heart. Those scars may remain a secret, tucked away out of the sight of others, but in many understandable ways they affect the function of that person from day to day.

Bette started her first year of teaching in the public schools full of ideas about what it took to be an outstanding teacher. She had no idea how much her students would teach her about the secrets of the heart.

She had taught preschool in her own home for several years. It was a Montessori preschool with an elite group of children enrolled. She applied to teach in an elementary school, but no jobs opened that year. Finally, just before school started in the fall, the assistant superintendent called to ask if she was willing to teach special-education English in a high school. He knew that her college minor was in special education. She was frightened but confident that if she offered discipline and a caring attitude, she would have few problems.

The students she taught that year bore no resemblance to her preschoolers. They came that first day dressed mostly in black and daring her to teach them. Their language was crude, and their demeanors were angry. She returned home after that first nightmarish day in tears, convinced that an outstanding special-education teacher was one who lived through the whole year.

But with administrative support, she set up a tough discipline policy. Once control was a part of her class, each student became a person, an individual with a secret. Why were they in special education? Why couldn't they read above a fifth-grade level?

For some, the secret was easy to figure out. Stacy could spell any word in the dictionary. But if you said, "The ball is red. What color is the ball?" he couldn't tell you. Stacy was a true special-education student, and the skills Bette had learned in school improved Stacy's abilities.

Robert sat with glazed eyes, his pupils dilated unevenly. His brain was full of drugs and alcohol. His mother had bathed his little brain with alcohol before birth and then had continued to give him access to it after birth. Bette couldn't teach him but tried to get him help for his abuse problem.

Jeff always did well on written assignments, but his test scores were so low that the disparity didn't make sense. He obviously had a secret that he wasn't telling. Bette had been teaching school only a quarter when he came to her and confessed his secret: he had cheated through almost twelve years of school. He didn't know how to read or write anything, although he could copy from five desks away. He was frightened. He was on the high school graduation roster and had no skills. Once Bette knew his secret, she could help him. A "payday" came for her after months of tutoring when Jeff said with tears in his eyes that he had ordered what he wanted to eat at McDonald's. He had always ordered what the person in front of him had ordered, but this time he had read and ordered what he wanted.

Kelly just plain didn't attend school, and obviously nobody really cared. School wasn't important to him, and he wasn't important to anyone. He was smart and was in special education only because he hadn't been to school. The best Bette could do for Kelly was make sure he knew that she cared.

Before the year was over, Bette had a new idea of what made an outstanding teacher. For Kelly, it was saying she cared; for Robert, finding a drug-treatment program; for Jeff, privately teaching him to read. And for some it was actually teaching what she was being paid to teach. Their secrets told her what they needed.

The following school year, she accepted a position to teach second grade at the elementary school just blocks from home. But even the seven-year-olds came with their secrets. They might have been as easy as "I wasn't ready to read in first grade, but now I'm ready" or "I learn better when I hear something than when I read it." Or as difficult as "My daddy's in prison for sexually abusing me, so I'm in my own world of hurt that doesn't leave me a lot of energy for learning."

One little boy's secret wasn't learned until the following year. The elementary school where Bette taught was originally built as an open school. The walls were portable and allowed noise to go from room to room. Each teacher worked hard to keep the noise level from reaching the next room.

John didn't seem to know what a whisper was. Each day, every student individually read phrases from a paper he or she had taken home and studied. John's voice carried to the next classroom daily as he read his homework. His volume control seemed to be stuck on extra-loud no matter how many times he was reminded to turn it down.

This problem wasn't solved in the second grade, and unfortunately it graduated to the third grade with John. His third-grade teacher complained several times to the other teachers about his volume.

Then one day John's volume was turned down. He spoke quietly at homework reading and when he answered questions. His third-grade teacher finally called him up to her desk. She said, "John, your voice is just right today. What has made the difference?"

He shrugged his shoulders, thought for a moment, and then said, "Maybe it's because my dad finally got his hearing aids." Out of necessity John had shouted at home for eight years. Now both teachers knew his secret.

Across the street from the local high school, Brother Jacobson taught seminary. One day after the devotional, Brother Jacobson stood and began to teach his seminary lesson for the day. As he got further into the lesson, he noticed that Art was leaning back in his seat with his eyes closed. He let out a quiet sigh of aggravation as he thought of the preparation time he had spent on the lesson. It was only third hour. He thought that Art should be more respectful than to sleep through his class. He kept quiet but fumed silently as Art appeared to slumber on.

Toward the end of class, Brother Jacobson was out of patience. He called Art's name. Art's eyelids rolled open as Brother Jacobson made a comment about his sleeping in class. Just then the door opened, distracting both of them. Art's mom was standing in the doorway. She asked if she could see her son for a moment. Brother Jacobson was pleased that she had chosen the very moment of Art's trouble to open the door. He walked to the back of the room and asked if he could help her with something. She explained that Art had called before class to tell her that he had one of his new contacts stuck in the back of his eye. Since she had worn contacts for years, Art had asked her to come to the school to help him get it out. Brother Jacobson blushed at the revealed secret. He now knew that closed eyes don't always mean someone is sleeping.

Secrets of the heart can be found beyond the school setting. They are present in every facet of our lives.

For instance, Boyd never ate with any of his coworkers. He always sat by himself away from the others. He never attended any of the company parties and never socialized with any of the men. Most of the workers at the plant knew little about him and had little chance to learn anything. Because of this, it didn't take long before many of the men at the plant began to think Boyd was antisocial or stuck-up. They started to make fun of him and plan ways to humiliate him. But Boyd was a good sport and just seemed to flow along with the practical jokes and rude comments.

One day, however, things changed. Robert and Jared decided to play a joke on Boyd by giving him a package during lunch. In the package they placed some apple cores, chicken bones, and potato peels. They whispered their secret around the plant until everyone but Boyd was anticipating a great laugh during lunch. At the beginning of the lunch hour, Robert made a general, loud announcement that all were to gather around. They shuffled Boyd to the front of the group and told him that all the men at the plant had chipped in and bought some special food for him. They all tried to keep straight faces as Boyd smiled shyly and reached for the package.

He hesitated, then with great difficulty he thanked them all and offered a word of apology. He told them that he was sorry for not eating with them and for not being more friendly. Then he divulged his secret. He explained that his wife had cancer and had been very ill for almost two years. All of their savings had been used to pay doctor bills, and most of his paycheck each week was used to keep up with the financial burden of his sick wife and their seven growing children.

"I'm sorry I haven't eaten with you," he continued with tears slowly rolling down his face, "but by the time I fix lunch for my wife and children each day, there isn't much to put in my lunch box. I guess I shouldn't have been embarrassed, but I was." He then reached down and began to open the package as he thanked all the men for their kindness and assured them that his family would really appreciate the food.

With Boyd's secret revealed, Robert and Jared and all the other men at the plant were filled with understanding. With a pang of guilt, Robert quickly grabbed the partially opened package and told John that this wasn't enough; they wanted to give more.

The next day, with the help of everybody in the plant, Boyd was given several boxes of food and an envelope filled with bills totaling three hundred dollars.

None of us are immune from misjudging the secrets of the heart. Bishop H. Burke Peterson of the Presiding Bishopric told about meeting a young man while attending a stake conference in another country. At the conclusion of the Saturday afternoon meeting with the stake presidency, there came a knock at the door. An envelope was handed to the stake president with Bishop Peterson's name on it. The letter inside introduced a young man who needed to see Bishop Peterson for a mission interview.

When the meeting with the stake presidency concluded, Bishop Peterson invited the young man in for the interview. Bishop Peterson's first look at the young man brought him nothing but shock. He couldn't believe this boy was being recommended to go on a mission. His clothes were wrinkled, he smelled of tobacco smoke, and he needed to shave. Rolled up in his hand was some sort of paperback book. Bishop Peterson thought to himself, *What could he offer in the service of the Master?*

But these thoughts all changed as Bishop Peterson began to learn the secrets of this young man's heart. He first felt something special as he shook hands with the prospective missionary. The feeling he felt sent a different message than what he was seeing. Next, as they sat down the young man began to excuse his appearance. He explained that he had just gotten off a bus after traveling thirteen hours from his home. He also explained he would be getting right back on the bus after the interview to return home. Knowing this simple secret, it didn't take Bishop Peterson long to know that the wrinkled clothes and tobacco smell were from the ride on the bus.

As the interview progressed, more secrets began to unfold. Bishop Peterson noticed that the paperback book was a well-read Book of Mormon. The young man explained that he had joined the Church three years before. When he joined the Church, his parents told him he was no longer welcome in their home and he was asked to leave and never return. After leaving home he had worked and attended school. He explained that he had saved enough money to pay for two years of service to the Master. He then pleaded with Bishop Peterson to allow him the great privilege of going on a mission. Feeling the strong affirmative voice of the Spirit, Bishop Peterson had no doubt this young man was going to be a powerful missionary. It is no wonder that the Spirit spoke yes to Bishop Peterson's soul. (See "As a Beacon on a Hill," *Ensign*, November 1974, p. 68.)

Bette found out that high school students have secrets and that second-graders have secrets. Brother Jacobson learned that not everything is as it appears. Robert and Jared learned that adults have secrets. Bishop Peterson learned that prospective missionaries can have secrets. They all learned that often we may not know what someone's secret is, but we need to be patient with the knowledge that if we knew, we'd understand.

Every person we meet has secrets. Some of those secrets are good, and some of those secrets are difficult. All of the secrets cause people to act in certain ways. These people are our brothers and sisters. As we are helping each other through life, remembering the hidden secrets of our hearts will help us all to be more patient and understanding.

Who am I to judge another
When I walk imperfectly?
In the quiet heart is hidden
Sorrow that the eye can't see.

—*Susan Evans McCloud*

2
The Way to Judge

DURING WORLD WAR II Boyd K. Packer, who later became a member of the Quorum of the Twelve Apostles, was transferred overseas from Langley Field, Virginia. The group he was with was transported in boxcars that had been made into makeshift sleeping cars. Their meals were served from a camp kitchen and cooked over an open fire in one of the cars.

On the first day of travel their luggage was separated from them, so they spent the next six days in the same clothes. During those six days they were unable to take a bath or wash their clothes. To make matters worse, it was July, which made it very hot and humid.

As they arrived in Los Angeles one Sunday morning, they were told that they would be free to leave the train for a few hours. Brother Packer and a few other men decided they wanted to use this break to get a good meal.

They found a fine restaurant and went inside. The restaurant was crowded, so they found themselves waiting in line. There were several civilians in the line dressed in their Sunday best. Brother Packer found himself standing next to several distinguished-looking ladies. One of them turned around and looked him over. She then said in a voice loud enough to attract the attention of everyone in the restaurant, "My! What filthy men!" (See Boyd K. Packer, *Teach Ye Diligently* [Salt Lake City: Deseret Book Company, 1975], pp. 31–32.)

The woman in the restaurant made a quick judgment of Brother Packer and his traveling companions. Her judgment was based solely on their smell and outward appearance. She knew nothing of their circumstances. All she knew was that they had offensive body odor and looked filthy.

While flying on a plane, Elder Carlos E. Asay of the Seventy learned a great lesson about judging others by their appearance. As he boarded the plane, his spirit was sagging and his mood was less than desirable. After he sat down he started to work on some pressing items he had to get done. The seat next to him was empty. He silently hoped that no one would take the seat so he wouldn't have to be bothered by conversation or other distractions.

One of the last people on the plane was a hairy and unkempt young man. He hurried onto the plane and took the last remaining seat—the one next to Elder Asay. Elder Asay was not happy with this new seating companion. The worldly-looking young man wanted to carry on a conversation, but Elder Asay ignored him.

The minutes seemed to drag by, and the man attempted conversation one more time. "I feel that I offend you, and I want to make an explanation," he said. "I'm from Canada, and I've been attending a mechanics seminar in Utah. The seminar concluded with a workshop, and I've been deep in grease and grime all day. And as you can see and smell, I didn't have time to shower or change clothes before catching the plane. I hope you will forgive me."

After the man revealed his secret, Elder Asay was ashamed that he had been so selfish and had prejudged this man by his appearance. He apologized to the man for his thoughts, and they had a beautiful gospel conversation. Before they landed in Chicago they were reading the scriptures together and conversing like old friends. They parted with the promise that the man would receive the missionaries. (See Carlos E. Asay, "The Spirit of Missionary Work," *Ensign*, November 1976, p. 43.)

A similar judgment was made by some members of a student ward at Brigham Young University. The sacrament meeting began on a note of excitement and curiosity. The bishopric had been changed the previous week, but the new second counselor had not been presented because he had been out of town. Everyone knew he would be presented during this week's sacrament meeting.

As people looked for who might be the new counselor, several noticed a man sitting in the congregation who had a full beard, very long hair, and a thick mustache. He didn't look like he belonged because his hair did not meet the dress standards of Brigham Young University. Most of the students made unkind remarks about this stranger and had shunned him during the meetings leading up to sacrament meeting.

At the beginning of sacrament meeting, to the surprise of the congregation the hairy man was called to the stand and presented as the new second counselor to the bishop.

The bishop then stood and stated, "It was very interesting as I sat through priesthood meeting and Sunday School this morning and watched you as you noticed this hairy young man sitting among us. I wondered what some of you were thinking and didn't need to wonder about others as they volunteered little comments here and there."

The bishop then explained that the man had special permission to wear his beard, mustache, and long hair because he was playing the part of John the Baptist in a new Church film. (See Allan K. Burgess and Max H. Molgard, *Stories That Teach Gospel Principles* [Salt Lake City: Bookcraft, 1989], pp. 15–16.)

A great lesson on judging was learned that day. Those in the congregation discovered that there is more to understanding a person than just his outward appearance. Many times our quick judgments of appearance are made because we don't want to be bothered or take the time to understand someone else. It may be our habit to size up people as we meet them. Are their habits of cleanliness as meticulous as ours? Is their clothing clean and wrinkle-free? Is their hair cut well, clean, and well groomed?

It may be a boost to our own egos to belittle others while elevating ourselves. Is he dirtier than I am? Are my clothes nicer? Is my hair cleaner?

Such a habit needs to be changed if we want to follow our Savior. In the Old Testament he gave us the difference between worldly judgment and eternal judgment when he said to Samuel, "Look not on his countenance, or on the height of his stature; because I have refused him: for the Lord seeth not as man seeth; for man looketh on the outward appearance, but the Lord looketh on the heart" (1 Samuel 16:7).

Yes, the Lord looketh on the heart. He is the only one who can clearly see every secret of our hearts. He knows every detail of every secret and compassionately understands our resulting actions.

In this mortal state, we are unable to see the secrets others harbor within. Without knowing all of those secrets, we cannot make a fair judgment. In fact the Lord says: "Judge not, that ye be not judged. For with what judgment ye judge, ye shall be judged: and with what measure ye mete, it shall be measured to you again." (Matthew 7:1–2.)

We know that we should not judge others. But in the following verse, the Lord continues with an explanation of the righteous judgment that he wants us to make: "And why beholdest thou the mote that is in thy brother's eye, but considerest not the beam that is in thine own eye?" (Matthew 7:3.)

We should not judge others, but we should judge ourselves. Why is judging ourselves so important? Because the Lord will never judge us against others, not in this earthly life nor in the eternities to come. We will be judged against our own best efforts according to our circumstances, what we have been given, and what we are doing with what we have been given.

It is a waste of our time to judge others, and Satan knows it. He revels in each sizing up of others because he knows that we will be distracted from the judgment that will make a difference in our eternal progression.

Instead of judging others with a lofty "I'm sure I read more scriptures than Sister Brown" or a belittling "I'll never be able to get up at four-thirty every morning to study the scriptures like Sister Jacobs," we should be judging ourselves with an "I'm doing better this week than I did last week—and next week I'll do even better." That is the kind of judgment that moves us toward exaltation.

One of the most beautiful parts of the Atonement is that, in applying it to our lives, each of us has an individual price to pay. We all want to find ourselves worthy of being in the celestial kingdom. The pathway to that kingdom is not at all like a marathon in which those who finish first are the winners. But each of us has our own pathway with individual curves and trials and blessings. The only absolute requirement is that we do our best with what we have been given.

The Savior will pay the rest, if we give all that we have. And all that we each personally have will always be different from all that anyone else has. Without knowing the secrets of another's heart, as our Savior does, we cannot even come close to making a fair judgment. And why should we? There is only one vote that will count, and his vote will be given with all the secrets taken into consideration and in the circle of his perfect love.

As we eliminate competition with others, we will find a whole new beautiful and diverse world out there. Eliminating competition frees us to find out what we can learn from each person we come in contact with.

Max Jr. was in tenth grade when he came home from school and announced to his mother, Bette, that he was going to try out for a part in the school musical. Tryouts were just three short days away, and full of the optimism he had always possessed, he queried, "Mom, will you teach me how to sing?"

Max had sat with the deacons since his voice had changed, and Bette realized that she hadn't heard Max sing for years. His childhood voice had certainly been nothing to brag about. But, she reasoned, surely the years had brought improvement. She thought that people were either born with a pretty voice or not, so she would know if he could sing the minute she played a song on the piano and had him follow along.

That idea failed miserably. There was never a match of Max's voice to the notes his mother played on the piano. In short, his voice was among the top contenders for the worst voice she had ever heard. But how could she break this fact to Max?

She looked into his expectant eyes and decided to try a new strategy. She would play just one note on the piano and have him match it with his voice. After fifteen minutes of trying, the match had not been made. Her stomach was in knots thinking about the humiliation they would feel if they shared his voice with others.

Not about to be totally discouraged, she decided that he could sing a note and she would match it with the piano. Once a match was made, she went down the scale and found that he had taken enough music lessons on his trumpet to know what the steps and half-steps sounded like. In this time-consuming manner, they would arrive at the first note of the chosen song, and he could proceed from there with semi-satisfactory results. Bette knew that they wouldn't be totally humiliated at tryouts if she prayed mightily that he could find the first note.

The day of tryouts, Max combined his lack of musical skills with the fact that he was nervous and sang his heart out as he missed every note they had practiced. Bette thought to herself that if she had been him, that would have been the last time anyone heard her sing in public. But Max was not discouraged. "I think I'd better take voice lessons if I ever want to be a lead in a school musical," he said.

Bette rolled her eyes and wondered where she would ever find a teacher who would have the patience to work with someone who would never be able to learn to sing.

She found that teacher in a woman named Jean Poyer. Jean had an amazing way of knowing where the sound needed to come from and how to progress step by step until her students could reach their full potential. Bette knew that Max's full potential wouldn't be wonderful, but she couldn't discourage him from trying. He started lessons the following week.

Months passed. Max worked diligently on his lessons, and Jean seemed to be pleased. Bette wrote out the monthly checks for the voice lessons and thought of how many other things the family could have spent that money on. It seemed a bit of a waste, but she was willing to appease Max, at least for a little while. In the meantime, she encouraged him to practice back in his bedroom behind a closed door. She didn't think her musical ear could handle too much up-close practice time.

For Mother's Day that year, Max wrote a song for his mom. He asked her to go for a ride in the truck, and there in the privacy of the cab he sang his heart out. With tears streaming down her cheeks, Bette was surprised at how much Max's voice had improved. The notes were a little flat here and there, but it was tolerable. And the music he had written coupled with the words of his heart remain as a memory that will be treasured always.

Max joined a singing group and practiced weekly for their spiritual sacrament meeting presentations. Bette went to watch and could hear an improvement with each passing week. He tried out for the school musical his junior year and got a part in the chorus.

With continued effort, the miracle unfolded. By the time tryouts came around for the annual musical during his senior year, Max was fully prepared. As he completed his solo for the tryouts, his drama coach kiddingly asked where he had hidden the tape recorder. Bette accompanied his tryout and left the stage with a lump in her throat, bursting with pride.

Max was not given the lead in the school musical that year. But he had a part that required a vocal solo and worked hard during rehearsals. *The Unsinkable Molly Brown* was the musical chosen that year. Then just ten days before opening night, the male lead decided that he couldn't pull it off. Even though his voice was full and beautiful, his inexperience with acting left him uncomfortable with the part of Johnny Brown. That afternoon, Bette returned home to find a note: "Dear Mom and Dad," it said, "I won't be home until late tonight, and you probably won't see me much for the next ten days. I'm Johnny Brown!"

On opening night, some people might have judged that although Max's acting ability was marvelous and his voice was nice, it wasn't the most beautiful voice they had ever heard in a high school musical. But those who knew what Max's leading role had entailed could only clap louder during the standing ovation on closing night.

Max Jr. taught us all a valuable lesson. We need to judge ourselves against our own best efforts. Then, as we work on our weaknesses day by day, we will see progress and find great rewards as we concentrate on the judgment that moves us towards exaltation.

$\mathcal{T}$herefore judge nothing before the time, until the Lord come, who both will bring to light the hidden things of darkness, and will make manifest the counsels of the hearts: and then shall every man have praise of God.

—*1 Corinthians 4:5*

3

The Real Light

SEVERAL YEARS AGO A YOUNG man was serving a mission. One day he was surprised and delighted to hear he was being transferred to a beautiful city famous for tailor-made suits. This young missionary had always dreamed of a dark-blue suit made just for him.

Soon after his transfer, he discovered a talented tailor living in his branch and was thrilled when the tailor said he would be happy to make the suit. The young missionary wasted no time in picking out the material for his suit. He went up and down the aisles of the shop until he found a bolt of the prettiest dark-blue material he had ever seen. He gave the material to the tailor and waited with great anticipation for the suit's completion.

It wasn't long before the tailor called him and told him the suit was ready. The missionary and his companion finished their tracting for the day and hurried over to the tailor's shop. As he took off the protective plastic from the suit, he was thrilled with the fine construction. A visit to the fitting room revealed a perfect fit. "This suit is wonderful!" he proclaimed as he paid and thanked the tailor. He and his companion left the shop and stepped out into the bright summer sun. As they began to walk down the street, the companion got the funniest look on his face. "Hey, Elder, check out your suit," he said as he stopped to point and gawk. The missionary's excitement melted as he looked at his reflection in a store window. The sun's telling rays showed that the suit wasn't dark blue at all. It was the most horrible shade of purple anyone could imagine. In a flash of recognition the missionary realized he had never seen the true color of the material before he handed the bolt of fabric to the tailor. The drab, artificial light of the shop had hidden the dreadful purple hue. In a rush of embarrassment, the missionary returned to his apartment, removed the suit, and never wore it again.

So it is with life. Things are not always as they appear. Many of the judgments we make and perceptions we have of people come after we have considered them in artificial light. The Son is the only source of true light. Remember, the drab, artificial light of our mortal lives dulls the truth of all things. Things are not always as they appear.

Brother Larkin was a seminary teacher in a small Utah community. One day as he drove along a deserted country road, his thoughts were interrupted by movement off to the side of the road. Curious, he stopped to take a closer look. His searching gaze fell upon an older man struggling to climb out of a ditch. Brother Larkin put his car in park and rushed to give the man assistance. The man's inebriated movements soon revealed the problem. The man was drunk. Slowing his pace, Brother Larkin asked the man if he could help him. The man, still struggling, mumbled something about needing to get to town. Brother Larkin told him that he would be glad to give him a ride. He helped the man out of the ditch and over to his car and started toward town.

The drive to town was a ten-minute trip. As they started down the road, Brother Larkin asked the man, "What's your name?" That simple leading question began a flood of talk that lasted the entire ten minutes. The man poured out the secrets of his heart to Brother Larkin. By the time they got to the outskirts of town, Brother Larkin knew why this man was drunk alongside the road. Life had been hard and had left many scars.

Entering town, Brother Larkin asked the man where he wanted to go. He said he wanted to go to the local bar. Brother Larkin asked him if he was sure that was where he wanted to go. He said, "Yes, there are some people there that can take care of me."

They arrived at the bar and pulled into the parking lot. When the car stopped, the man thanked Brother Larkin for being so kind. "I appreciate your help," he said. "You're a good man. Come on in and let me buy you a drink." Brother Larkin's smile acknowledged the man's thoughtfulness. "I don't drink, but let me help you walk to your buddies," he said as he put the man's arm around his neck and they walked in tandem into the bar, where they parted with a handshake and good wishes.

Suppose someone had driven by the bar as Brother Larkin walked out of the bar. What would have been their conclusion? Would they have passed their incorrect observation on to others? Would the story have been embellished as it was passed on? Would Brother Larkin's good influence built by years of teaching the youth have been put in jeopardy? If Brother Larkin had heard about the story and tried to explain himself, could he have possibly gathered back all of the scattered feathers of his plucked reputation?

Our Savior said: "Therefore all things whatsoever ye would that men should do to you, do ye even so to them: for this is the law and the prophets" (Matthew 7:12). Following his admonition means to refrain from passing on any story that would hurt another. If we question what we see, we should go to the source. That is the only place we will be able to see clearly, with perfect light.

Another story illustrating this concept was told by President N. Eldon Tanner of the First Presidency:

A retired man who worked in his garden early each day noticed that a milkman began stopping regularly each morning at the home of his neighbor across the street. He arrived just after the husband left for work and stayed a half hour or so. The attractive young housewife was a Primary teacher and was almost always in attendance at sacrament meetings.

After this pattern continued for several weeks, the man began to call it to the attention of the neighbors, expressing concern for the children she taught and the effect of her example. By the time he felt it his duty to report the situation to the bishop, news of the situation was widespread in the ward.

The bishop was disturbed over the whole affair and called the manager of the dairy to get the name of the delivery man and to inquire into his character. The manager approached the milkman and said tactfully, "I notice you have a new customer out on Lincoln Avenue. How did you get the lead?"

"Lead?" said the milkman. "That's my daughter. She fixes breakfast for me every morning, and my wife and I tend her children for her every Friday night. How's that for a deal?" ("'Nay, Speak No Ill,'" *Ensign*, March 1973, p. 2.)

Imagine the feathers that had to be retrieved after that fiasco. Nothing can fix the hurt imposed or call back the time wasted passing judgments made in artificial light.

To complicate those judgments further, none of us see through the same eyes. Our perceptions are tinted by life's experiences. Those experiences give us each a different slant or perspective than will be seen by others.

Consider a man with the following characteristics: age thirty, six feet tall, 175 pounds, brown hair, clean shaven, wearing slacks, sports coat, and no tie.

Now let's consider how each of the following people might describe the man:

A six-year-old boy: "He was real big and real old."

A man with a small head and large nose: "He had a large head and smelled funny."

A man from the Middle East: "He was a westerner."

A twenty-two-year-old woman: "He had the prettiest brown hair and a cute nose. He was a real knockout."

A six-foot-six rancher from Montana: "He was a scrawny, little, short-haired twerp from back East."

A six-foot-eight college basketball player: "He was well dressed, short, a little overweight, with a lot of hair."

An eighty-seven-year-old man: "He was a healthy, good-looking young kid, but he was dressed rather shabbily."

As you can see, many of our judgments and interpretations of what's going on in the world around us have to do with our perspective. Our perspectives may be in balance with the true light, or they may sway the truth to the other side of the spectrum.

Our Savior Jesus Christ is the one who has true perspective. He knows all of our secrets. He knows the pain, the scars, the hurt. He felt them all in the Garden of Gethsemane. He is the one with the true light, and his warning on judging others without the benefit of that light is simple: "For with what judgment ye judge, ye shall be judged: and with what measure ye mete, it shall be measured to you again" (Matthew 7:2).

This is followed with an admonition by one who knows of the universal tendencies of mortals then and now: "And why beholdest thou the mote that is in thy brother's eye, but considerest not the beam that is in thine own eye? Or how wilt thou say to thy brother, Let me pull out the mote out of thine eye; and, behold, a beam is in thine own eye? Thou hypocrite, first cast out the beam out of thine own eye; and then shalt thou see clearly to cast out the mote out of thy brother's eye." (Matthew 7:3–5.)

As we work step by step to perfect ourselves, we will be blessed with increased portions of the Lord's true light. With that light, we will be in the position to serve others through love and example as we help them come to him. Helping with love, not judgment or criticism, will allow us to become one of the chosen that he was speaking to when he said: "Ye are the light of the world. A city that is set on an hill cannot be hid. Neither do men light a candle, and put it under a bushel, but on a candlestick; and it giveth light unto all that are in the house. Let your light so shine before men, that they may see your good works, and glorify your Father which is in heaven." (Matthew 5:14–16.)

Shall not God search this out? for he knoweth the secrets of the heart.

—*Psalm 44:21*

4
What's Their Secret?

THERE IS A GAME WE PLAY CALLED "What's Their Secret?" The rules for the game are simple:

1. When you meet or see someone who is doing something that causes you to react in a negative way, stop and ask yourself, "What's their secret?"

2. Once you have asked the question, then make a list of possible answers. Note: none of these answers may be the real answer, but they may stop you from making a quick, unfair, or wrong judgment.

3. After you have made the list, ask yourself how Jesus would deal with this person and their actions.

Here is an example of how to play the game:

A festive Christmas morning opening presents with our children had been concluded with a quick lunch and cleanup. Then, because it was tradition, we piled into the car for the 100-mile trip to Grandma's house. The highway was a bustle of activity. We passed several gift-laden cars full of college students heading home and other families driving down the road, obviously anticipating their family get-togethers. The radio filled our van with Christmas carols, and we joined in until our singing faded as we noticed the blue and red flashing lights of two highway patrol cars several hundred yards ahead. We knew there had been an accident, and we said a silent prayer that the happiness of Christmas wouldn't be ruined by tragedy. As we slowly approached, we were relieved to see an old, rusty car in front of the patrol cars fully intact. Our curious gawking led us to the front of the rusty car, where a disheveled man stood by the officers. His head was down, and one officer was writing on his ticket pad. It didn't take us very long to put two and two together as we saw an open beer can next to a case of beer on the hood of the old car.

At first, we were thoroughly disgusted. Imagine, driving drunk on Christmas Day. What kind of man would put other lives in peril on a holiday? The question still hung in the air as we began to ask, "What's his secret? Why would someone be alone on Christmas Day? Why would he be drinking?"

Our sad choices of possible answers to these questions changed our thoughts of anger and disgust to sympathy and charity. A new spirit and attitude engulfed us. We hadn't asked the man why he was off the road that Christmas afternoon. We had just brainstormed possibilities. Yes, his drunk driving was wrong, but our reaction had turned from condemnation and judgment to positive thoughts of charity and understanding. Seldom is a life changed by harsh judgment or condemnation, but charity and understanding can become a life-changing habit.

Students of psychology will remember Ivan Pavlov, who tried to prove that a certain reaction can be tied to a certain stimulus. He noticed that when he fed his dogs, they would see the food and salivate in expectation. The stimulus was food, and the reaction was salivation. He added a bell to the situation by ringing the bell as he fed the dogs. Several days later he rang the bell, and without the stimulus of food the dogs salivated. It was an automatic reaction. Many of us have become like Pavlov's dogs. We see a situation and immediately react with a negative judgment. It is something we do automatically without thinking. This reaction taints the happiness of our lives and the happiness of others as we judge and react multiple times daily.

Elder Marvin J. Ashton of the Quorum of the Twelve Apostles taught the difference between acting and reacting. One day while he was walking with a friend, they passed a neighbor working in his front yard. Elder Ashton's friend raised his arm in friendly greeting and gave the neighbor a happy hello. The man didn't look up and continued working with no response. Elder Ashton said, "He is an old grouch today, isn't he?" His friend's surprising response was, "Oh, he is always that way." Elder Ashton asked, "Then why are you so friendly to him?" The friend responded with, "Why not? Why should I let him decide how I am going to act?" (See Conference Report, October 1970, p. 36.)

So it should be with all of us. Instead of reacting negatively to what people say and do, we should act in a positive, constructive way. Remembering that there is probably a very good reason the person is doing what he or she is doing will help us to be positive. We must remember that most of the time the reason won't be obvious but will be a secret hidden behind a callous or angry exterior.

That is why the "What's Their Secret?" game is so valuable. It teaches us to act instead of react. When something happens, we should assume the positive instead of the negative. One example is a lesson learned one day by a seminary teacher named Brother Jordan.

A student of Brother Jordan's named Julie had missed his class three days in a row. Brother Jordan was more aggravated than worried. Julie had missed several classes in the past without good excuses. Consequently, Brother Jordan assumed the negative. He concluded that she had been truant. As she entered the classroom door the morning of the fourth day, Brother Jordan sarcastically asked, "So, Julie, where have you been for the last three days?" Julie quietly replied, "Didn't you hear? I fell out of the back of a truck Monday night."

Brother Jordan immediately transformed his feelings and conversation to concern and empathy instead of condemnation. He chastised himself for his negative judgment and vowed that he would be more charitable toward his students and not assume anything until he knew the facts.

Another important thing to remember about acting instead of reacting is that someday we may be the one being misjudged. It is likely that this will eventually happen to all of us. When it does, our positive actions and understanding toward those who have misjudged us can have a profound effect upon our lives and the lives of others. A good example of this is found in the Old Testament in 1 Samuel 1–2.

A man by the name of Elkanah had two wives. Their names were Hannah and Peninnah. Peninnah had been able to have children, but Hannah had been barren. Hannah's inability to conceive caused her a great deal of sorrow.

Every year Elkanah and his family went to Shiloh to worship and offer sacrifice to the Lord. One year, Hannah was consumed with her grief because of her inability to have children. She rose one morning and went to the temple of the Lord. There she prayed with all of her heart and shed many tears. She made a commitment to the Lord that if she was blessed with a child she would dedicate him to his service.

As she offered this humble prayer in front of the temple, Eli the priest saw her. Seeing her lack of emotional control, he immediately judged that she was drunk and chided her for her public display by saying, "How long wilt thou be drunken? put away thy wine from thee" (1 Samuel 1:14).

Putting ourselves in Hannah's position, we can feel how hurt she must have been. She had gone to the temple with a heavy heart only to be further reprimanded by the high priest. What would your reaction be? Many would have left the temple filled with bitterness and vowed never to return.

Hannah teaches us all a lesson on how to handle those who judge without knowing our secrets. Realizing Eli's misunderstanding, she explained what she was doing at the temple, that she wasn't drinking but in her anguish was pouring out her soul to the Lord. With this understanding, Eli promised her that her prayer would be answered and that the Lord would remember her and her affliction.

Hannah's prayer was answered, as she and Elkanah were blessed with a son, whom they named Samuel. Hannah kept her promise and dedicated Samuel to the Lord for his service. Samuel became one of the great prophets of Israel.

If Hannah had been offended by what Eli had said to her as she prayed in front of the temple, she may have missed the beautiful blessing of having a prophet for a son. Her choice of action led to a further blessing of having three more sons and two daughters.

The problem between Eli and Hannah was a simple misunderstanding. Once Eli understood Hannah's secret, he responded positively. Satan loves to destroy us and our relationships by using this very effective tool called misunderstanding. Most of the time, misunderstanding is a direct result of improper judging. We automatically jump to conclusions without knowing all of the secrets. A real understanding of people and their secrets can come only with patience and positive action. Quick judgments and negative reaction will only increase the problem and destroy relationships.

We have all made the same kind of mistake that Brother Jordan and Eli made. The Lord counseled us how we should handle such a mistake when he gave us the parable of the lost coin: "Either what woman having ten pieces of silver, if she lose one piece, doth not light a candle, and sweep the house, and seek diligently till she find it? And when she hath found it, she calleth her friends and her neighbours together, saying, Rejoice with me; for I have found the piece which I had lost." (Luke 15:8–9.)

When we misjudge or offend someone, we should be quick to "sweep the house." The longer a "lost coin" is left unattended, the more it becomes hidden and eventually may fall completely through the cracks, making a recovery next to impossible. We all know those in the Church who have been lost coins that could have been swept up quite easily immediately after a misunderstanding. But the sweeping was neglected, and years later they have fallen far away from the mainstream of the Church.

That's because Satan clearly understands the power of hate caused by misunderstandings and misjudgment. Frederick Babbel tells of an experience he had after World War II in Europe. He said while he was giving a talk to Church members in London, he had a keen realization of a power surging through his body. Describing the power later, he said it was like a railway engineer "at the throttle of a powerful locomotive." He felt that he "needed only to turn the throttle to unleash unlimited divine power." It was no wonder to him, therefore, that afterwards, when he was asked to bless two of the members present, he felt that "there was no limit to the blessing each could receive."

The first was "a sister in her seventh month of pregnancy who had been bleeding so profusely that both she and her husband feared she might lose the baby prematurely." As Brother Babbel confirmed the anointing, he again felt the tremendous surge of power that he had previously felt and knew that she would be healed immediately. She later confirmed that she had been healed from that moment.

The second person was a three-year-old boy from Scotland who had been a deaf-mute since birth. His parents had brought him to London for a special blessing. After the boy had been anointed with oil, Brother Babbel placed his hands upon the boy's head to seal the anointing. As he did so, he felt the Lord's power in such abundance that there was no question in his mind that the boy would be healed instantly.

Before he could say a word, he was told by the Spirit, "This young boy could be healed this very night if his parents would lose the hatred which they have in their hearts." He was decidedly shocked and troubled, because he had never before met this family and did not want to question their attitude. But he was restrained from sealing the anointing.

After a moment's pause, he removed his hands from the boy's head and said to the parents, "What is it that you hate so deeply?"

They looked startled. Then the husband said, "We can't tell you."

Brother Babbel told them he didn't need to know. He then explained to them as he placed his hands upon their son's head that he had been assured that their son might be healed that very night and restored to wholeness if they would lose the hatred which they had in their hearts.

After some troubled glances back and forth between the couple, the husband again spoke. "Well, if that is the case," he said, "our son will have to go through life as he is, because we won't give up our hating!" (See Frederick W. Babbel, *On Wings of Faith* [Salt Lake City: Bookcraft, 1972], pp. 159–61.)

It is hard to understand how anyone could hang on to hate so tightly that their child would be denied the blessing of health. This is a sorrowful example of how powerful hate can be and what it can do to destroy the good things in our lives. The frightening thing about hate is that it can be passed on to taint posterity for generations.

An example of this is the trouble that arose between Nephi and his brothers Laman and Lemuel. They accused Nephi falsely and taught their children to hate Nephi and those who followed him. They in turn taught their children, until hundreds of years later the hate caused by one family had spread to a nation of people. This is evidenced when Ammon and Lamoni meet Lamoni's father, who said: "Whither art thou going with this Nephite, who is one of the children of a liar?"

After this question, Lamoni explained that he and Ammon were on their way to free Ammon's brothers who were in prison. "And now when Lamoni had rehearsed unto him all these things, behold, to his astonishment, his father was angry with him, and said: Lamoni, thou art going to deliver these Nephites, who are sons of a liar.

Behold, he [Nephi] robbed our fathers; and now his children are also come amongst us that they may, by their cunning and their lyings, deceive us, that they again may rob us of our property." (See Alma 20:10–13.) Because of the false traditions of hate, Lamoni's father automatically assumed that all Nephites were liars.

Not long ago we had the privilege of having a couple and their daughter in our home for dinner. They had recently moved to the United States from Moscow, Russia. We spent a fascinating evening with this wonderful family as they told us of their homeland and the loved ones they had left there. After their departure we were left with a disheartened feeling of having been deceived. All of our lives we had been raised with a tradition of hate towards and fear of Russia and its people. The media had painted a picture of a cold, unfriendly, hateful populace. These Russians were warm, friendly, and full of love. This experience taught us a valuable lesson about judging people based on false traditions and teachings. We should remember the words of the Savior: "Judge not according to your traditions, but judge righteous judgment" (JST, John 7:24).

Remembering to acknowledge secrets when judging or being judged can bring the Spirit into our lives and may enrich the lives of our children and their children. A habit of playing "What's Their Secret?" can positively transform our lives and spread to the happiness of others.

What have we? Our time. Spend it as you will. Time is given to you; and when this is spent to the best possible advantage for promoting truth upon the earth, it is placed to our account, and blessed are you; but when we spend our time in idleness and folly it will be placed against us.

—Brigham Young

5
Time Wasted

Time: TWELVE MONTHS IN A YEAR, thirty days in a month, twenty-four hours in a day, sixty minutes in an hour, sixty seconds in a minute—and no one knows how many years in a lifetime. We get only one chance at our time on earth. What are we going to do with that preparatory time? How are we going to fill our minutes, hours, and days? We are promised, "He who is faithful and wise in time is accounted worthy to inherit the mansions prepared for him of my Father" (D&C 72:4), and we read that "this life became a probationary state; a time to prepare to meet God" (Alma 12:24).

How are we preparing? Are we being faithful and wise with our time, or are we wasting part of our days? What things rob our eternal progress? Our time may be wasted in several areas. When we delete those areas from our lives, the time saved will leave plenty of building, preparatory time.

Big chunks of our time are wasted in wafting back and forth making certain decisions, asking ourselves whether we should do something or not.

Tithing was the subject of the lesson in the sixteen- to eighteen-year-old Sunday School class. The class was filled with typical teenagers, sprinkled with a few vocal, assertive students. They loved a good debate and had enjoyed bantering about many gospel topics in the past. This particular Sunday was no different. The lesson had started off calmly enough. Then Barbie commented, "Tithing is not a choice," and that had started an interesting discussion. "Of course it's a choice," someone else said. "Every time someone makes money, they can choose what to do with it. They can pay tithing or they can spend it all on something else."

Barbie's insightful reply taught us all how to save a lot of time and energy. "For me, tithing isn't a choice. It was a choice a long time ago. I decided that I would always pay my tithing. Now I don't have to waste my time making that same decision over and over again. When I make money, I always know I will pay my tithing. There is no other choice."

The prophet Joshua made a similar decision when the children of Israel were preparing to enter the promised land. He stated to those present: "And if it seem evil unto you to serve the Lord, choose you this day whom ye will serve; whether the gods which your fathers served that were on the other side of the flood, or the gods of the Amorites, in whose land ye dwell: but as for me and my house, we will serve the Lord" (Joshua 24:15).

Joshua had made the decision to serve the Lord. He didn't have to struggle making the choice over and over again. He had already made his decision.

Consider how much time we waste making some decisions. Can we make global decisions that finalize many of our choices? Can some of our actions simply be a follow-through on previous decisions? This is an effective tool in mastering most gospel principles.

Think about saying your prayers, reading your scriptures, staying morally clean, and keeping the Word of Wisdom. A person who makes the choice to never drink an alcoholic beverage doesn't have to decide when faced with a smooth-talking peer or a socially awkward situation. They already know what the answer will be.

Now consider a life-changing global choice that will multiply our precious allotment of time. We may never encounter a drug pusher or find ourselves facing a temptation to commit a grievous sin of immorality. But we will all, without exception, be faced with the choice of spending our time judging others or filling that time giving them kind attention. Make the choice now that you will not waste your time judging others. Finding fault is easy, but help and understanding take charity and time. President Gordon B. Hinckley emphasized this when he said: "I plead for understanding among our people, for a spirit of tolerance toward one another, and for forgiveness. All of us have far too much to do to waste our time and energies in criticism, faultfinding, or the abuse of others. The Lord has commanded this people, saying: 'Strengthen your brethren in all your conversation, in all your prayers, in all your exhortations, and in all your doings.' This is the commandment, stated unequivocally; and then follows this marvelous promise: 'And behold, and lo, I am with you to bless you and deliver you forever.' (D&C 108:7–8.)" ("Faith: The Essence of True Religion," *Ensign*, November 1981, p. 6.)

Imagine, the Savior will forever bless those who take the time to look deeper into the hearts of individuals who need our help and understanding. Elder Marvin J. Ashton of the Quorum of the Twelve Apostles related the story of one young woman who was serving in a stake Relief Society presidency. During a presidency meeting one morning, she lost her temper. At the time she was laboring under the pressure of an especially challenging project. Elder Ashton explained further:

> The cause of her unhappiness had little to do with the question at hand and was related more to the fact that at the time she was laboring under intense home pressure on a major task and was feeling frustrated and frazzled. Afterwards, she was embarrassed at her behavior and immediately called to apologize for her outburst. Her friends in the presidency were generous and told her not to think another thing about it. Still she wondered if they might think less of her, now that they'd seen her at less than her best. But that evening the doorbell rang around dinnertime, and there stood the

other members of the presidency with dinner in hand. "We knew when you lost your cool this morning that you must just be worn out. We thought a little supper might help. We want you to know we love you." The young woman was amazed. In spite of her outburst that morning, her friends were there to offer support rather than criticism. Rather than seize the opportunity to bash her, they were filled with the spirit of charity. ("The Tongue Can Be a Sharp Sword," *Ensign*, May 1992, p. 20.)

It's a wonderful story. But would it have found its way into the *Ensign* if we would have been placed in similar circumstances? Or would we have gloated at the humanness of the member of the presidency who had always seemed to set a wonderful example? Would our afternoon have been spent calling our friends to let them know the morning's less-desirable details or spent charitably fixing her dinner?

Think of the power and extra time that can come into our lives if we spend the time offering assistance to those we easily could have wasted time judging. The following is a good example of what can happen when such a resolve is part of our lives:

A young mother on an overnight flight with a two-year-old daughter was stranded by bad weather in Chicago airport without food or clean clothing for the child and without money. She was two months pregnant and threatened with miscarriage, so she was under doctor's instructions not to carry the child unless it was essential. Hour after hour she stood in one line after another, trying to get a flight to Michigan. The terminal was noisy, full of tired, frustrated, grumpy passengers, and she heard critical references to her crying child and to her sliding her child along the floor with her foot as the line moved forward. No one offered to help with the soaked, hungry, exhausted child. Then, the woman later reported, "someone came towards us and with a kindly smile said, 'Is there something I could do to help you?' With a grateful sigh I accepted his offer. He lifted my sobbing little daughter from the cold floor and lovingly held her to him while he patted her gently on the back. He asked if she could chew a piece of gum. When she was settled down, he carried her with him and said something kindly to the others in the line ahead of me, about how I needed their help. They seemed to agree and then he went up to the ticket counter [at the front of the line] and made arrangements with the clerk for me to be put on a flight leaving shortly. He walked with us to a bench, where we chatted a moment, until he was assured that I would be fine. He went on his way. About a week later I saw a picture of Apostle Spencer W. Kimball and recognized him as the stranger in the airport." (Edward L. Kimball and Andrew E. Kimball, Jr., *Spencer W. Kimball* [Salt Lake City: Bookcraft, 1977], p. 334.)

President Kimball didn't waste his time wondering why the mother was not taking care of her child but instead went to work. The disapproving thoughts, criticism, and lack of action on the part of those in the airport were a wasted effort.

Have you ever sat in a sacrament meeting listening to a speaker and had your mind occupied with how he was dressed, his voice, or his grammar? Our minds can think of only one thing at a time. Are we shooing good things out while we critique the speaker? Are we robbing ourselves of the message we were supposed to hear?

President Heber J. Grant told of an experience he had when he was a teenager. While listening to Bishop Millen Atwood preach a sermon in the Thirteenth Ward, he noticed that he was making some grammatical errors in his talk. At the time he was studying grammar and had been given the assignment to take to class sentences that were not grammatically correct along with the corrections. He wrote down Bishop Atwood's first sentence, smiled, and said: "I am going to get here tonight, during the thirty minutes that Brother Atwood speaks, enough material to last me for the entire winter in my night school grammar class."

As he contemplated making his corrections, he listened to Bishop Atwood's sermon. "But," recalled President Grant, "I did not write anything more after that first sentence—not a word; and when Millen Atwood stopped preaching, tears were rolling down my cheeks, tears of gratitude and thanksgiving that welled up in my eyes because of the marvelous testimony which that man bore of the divine mission of Joseph Smith."

More than sixty-five years after that experience, President Grant said that the sensations and feelings that he felt then were just as vivid as the day he heard the sermon. He said that he would no more have thought of using the sentences in which Bishop Atwood had made grammatical mistakes than he would have thought of "standing up in a class and profaning the name of God."

President Grant further said: "During all the years that have passed since then, I have never been shocked or annoyed by grammatical errors or mispronounced words on the part of those preaching the gospel. I have realized that it was like judging a man by the clothes he wore, to judge the spirit of a man by the clothing of his language."

From then on President Grant was impressed more by a speaker's message of inspiration than by his or her language. He taught: "After all is said and done there are a great many who have never had the opportunity to become educated so far as speaking correctly is concerned. Likewise there are many who have never had an opportunity in the financial battle of life to accumulate the means whereby they could be clothed in an attractive manner. I have endeavored, from that day to this, and have been successful in my endeavor, to judge men and women by the spirit they have; for I have learned absolutely, that it is the Spirit that giveth life and understanding, and not the letter. The letter killeth." (See *Gospel Standards*, comp. G. Homer Durham [Salt Lake City: *Improvement Era*, 1941], pp. 294–96.)

Elder Jacob de Jager of the Seventy said, "The faults and short-comings we see in the members of our own ward or branch are of less consequence to us than one of the smallest in ourselves" ("Climbing to Higher Spirituality," *Ensign*, May 1993, p. 76).

Elder Marvin J. Ashton gave us the key to filling our time righteously when he said, "Meaningful progress can be made only when all of us can cast the motes out of our own eyes, leave judgment to our Father in Heaven, and lose ourselves in righteous living" ("Pure Religion," *Ensign*, November 1982, p. 64).

Among the most powerful tools for building or destroying others are the words we speak. Think about the things you remember people having said to you over the years. The negative things that have been said tend to hang with us for a long time. While typing her mother's autobiography, Bette was amazed that over seventy years hadn't erased unkind words spoken by a first-grade teacher.

President Gordon B. Hinckley counseled: "Restrain your tongues in criticism of others. It is so easy to find fault. It is so much nobler to speak constructively." ("'Charity Never Faileth,'" *Ensign*, November 1981, p. 98.) How well we follow this counsel will be a real measure of who we are. Elder ElRay L. Christiansen, Assistant to the Quorum of the Twelve Apostles, said, "The more perfect one becomes, the less he is inclined to speak of the imperfection of others" (in Conference Report, April 1956, p. 114).

Using the Savior as our standard, consider this statement by Elder Ashton: "At no time did Jesus Christ encourage us to spend time participating in damaging, destructive criticism. His message was to encourage us to seek, learn, and share all that is praiseworthy and of value as we associate with our fellowmen. Only those who are vindictive and cantankerous participate in ferreting out and advertising the negative and unsavory." ("Pure Religion," *Ensign*, November 1982, p. 63.)

Conversely, we also hold on to and savor words that feel good. Bette walked into her parents' darkened bedroom one evening to say good night. They didn't see or hear her enter, so they continued their positive conversation about her. They spoke of her talents and their pride. Bette hadn't felt too positive about herself during her high school years. Later, when discouragement set in, she had the details of that conversation to bouy her up. It's been twenty-six years and she can still feel the magic of that evening.

That kind of magic can fill our lives and be passed on to others. It will not only replace the wasted negative, judging times but will fill our lives with happiness and spiritual growth. That feeling is always contagious. It will fill our lives and rub off on our acquaintances, friends, and most important of all, our families.

That there should be no schism in the body; but that the members should have the same care one for another.

And whether one member suffer, all the members suffer with it.

—*1 Corinthians 12:25–26*

6

Shearing the Sheep

ALL OF US BENEFIT FROM THE wool sheared from sheep. An individual sheep can provide enough wool to supply clothing for several people. But the heavy wool must be removed at the right time of year. It doesn't take a lot of thought to know that sheep can't be sheared in the middle of winter. Just like many other animals, sheep need a heavy coat to provide warmth and protection during the winter months. If you were to remove that woolly protection during the coldest part of winter, the sheep would not survive.

There is another type of shearing, figuratively speaking: the shearing of human beings.

Mike and Janet married with high hopes of having a large family. After they waited a few years for the first blessed event, tests revealed they wouldn't be able to have children. Overcoming their disappointment was difficult. But after searching their options, they concluded they could still have their large family. They would adopt their children. Over the next few years, six precious bundles entered their home. Those children grew and were the center of Mike and Janet's life. They spent quality time with them, taught them the gospel, and did all in their knowledge and power to raise a righteous family.

Three of those children had very little spacing between their birthdays. They began school within a year of each other. They were great friends, but as they entered their teenage years they began to make bad choices together. They rebelled against all Mike and Janet had taught them and began to get into a great deal of trouble. The phone rang off the hook. The school called on a regular basis to inform the frustrated parents of their children's delinquent behavior. The calls began to pour in from the police, neighbors, Church members, relatives, and friends.

The more their three children strayed, the harder Mike and Janet worked to help them. Even though they found themselves being drained both physically and emotionally, they were unwilling to give up on their wayward children. They went through several trying years before things seemed to get better.

Many years later, Janet confided an interesting commentary on this trying experience. She told a friend that until this experience she had never questioned her self-worth. However, during those difficult years she found herself questioning not only her parenting skills but her worth as an individual. Had she done something terribly wrong in raising her children? How did others make parenting look so easy? As she had listened to friends gossip about others' stray sheep, she knew she and her family were at the top of the did-you-hear list. The deeper she sank into despair, the more often the telephone screamed. The schools, the Church, the neighbors all had reports.

"You know," she recalled, "every call I received during those years was someone letting me know how bad my kids were. The phone would ring and my stomach would churn. I was doing my best, and I didn't know what else to do. What I needed was an understanding heart or listening ear. Yet not one person ever asked me how they could help."

We are all so quick to make judgments and point critical fingers. Janet had been sheared by her three children and then others had called and turned on the cold air.

Elder Hans B. Ringger of the Seventy said: "It is not for us to judge those who might be confused or who have not the strength to change. What they need is our understanding and support." (" 'Choose You This Day,' " *Ensign*, May 1990, p. 26.)

Janet had discovered what Brigham Young was talking about when he said: "I frequently think of the difference between the power of God and the power of the Devil. To illustrate, here is a structure in which we can be seated comfortably, protected from the heat of summer or the cold of winter. Now, it required labor, mechanical skill and ingenuity and faithfulness and diligence to erect this building, but any poor, miserable fool or devil can set fire to it and destroy it. That is just what the Devil can do, but he never can build anything. The difference between God and the Devil is that God creates and organizes, while the whole study of the Devil is to destroy." (*Discourses of Brigham Young*, sel. John A. Widtsoe [Salt Lake City: Deseret Book Company, 1978], p. 69.)

This truth is reiterated in section 10 of the Doctrine and Covenants. Joseph Smith had temporarily entrusted 116 pages of manuscript from the book of Lehi to Martin Harris. When those pages were subsequently lost, Joseph had the plates and the ability to translate taken from him for a season. When the plates were returned and he was allowed to resume the work of translation, the Lord gave Joseph a review of what had happened and instructed him not to retranslate the portion of the plates that the 116 pages of manuscript had come from. In this revelation the Lord highlights the focus of Satan's work:

Behold, they have sought to *destroy* you; yea, even the man in whom you have trusted has sought to *destroy* you.

And for this cause I said that he is a wicked man, for he has sought to take away the things wherewith you have been entrusted; and he has also sought to *destroy* your gift. . . .

And, on this wise, the devil has sought to lay a cunning plan, that he may *destroy* this work; . . .

Therefore we [evil designers] will *destroy* him, and also the work; and we will do this that we may not be ashamed in the end, and that we may get glory of the world. . . .

Satan stirreth them up, that he may lead their souls to *destruction*.

And thus he has laid a cunning plan, thinking to *destroy* the work of God; but I will require this at their hands, and it shall turn to their shame and condemnation in the day of judgment. . . .

Yea, he saith unto them: Deceive and lie in wait to catch, that ye may *destroy*; behold, this is no harm. And thus he flattereth them, and telleth them that it is no sin to lie that they may catch a man in a lie, that they may *destroy* him. . . .

And thus he goeth up and down, to and fro in the earth, seeking to *destroy* the souls of men. (D&C 10:6–7, 12, 19, 22–23, 25, 27; emphasis added.)

As demonstrated in these verses, the hub of Satan's work is the destruction of anything good. God's work is just the opposite, as we're taught by the Lord in the same section of the Doctrine and Covenants: "And now, behold, according to their faith in their prayers will I bring this part of my gospel to the knowledge of my people. Behold, I do not bring it to destroy that which they have received, but to *build* it up. . . . Now I do not say this to destroy my church, but I say this to *build* up my church." (D&C 10:52, 54; emphasis added.)

God's work is to build his children. Satan's work is to destroy.

If we are true disciples of our Savior, our work should be to build our spirit brothers and sisters. When his work is our work, we are truly his disciples.

A good boost to our discipleship can be given in the words and intent of our prayers. A humorous story will illustrate:

Two young brothers were picked up by the police one Saturday night. They were basically good kids but were caught doing some mischievous things. The policeman who picked them up knew the boys and their father. He chuckled quietly to himself as he locked them up in the cell and walked to the office to place a call to their father. He knew the jail time they would spend while waiting for their father to pick them up would provide a valuable lesson. Their father also saw the value of the lesson. They had been stepping over the line at home. He reasoned that an entire night would really drive the lesson home. He told his friend he would pick them up after church the next afternoon.

Sunday morning, two repentant boys looked at the clock on the wall and knew their family was sitting in church. The more they talked about it, the more wistful they became. One of the brothers cautiously asked if there was any reason they couldn't have church right there in the jail. It was a welcome idea, and one brother agreed to say the prayer and the other to give a talk. The brother assigned the prayer addressed Heavenly Father and then said, "We are so grateful to be here today. Please bless all those who are not here this week that they may be here next week."

This humorous story illustrates how we sometimes forget to put our thoughts in gear before we pray. Of course it is nice to remember those who are not with us or those who may be sick or troubled. But how much better it would be for us to think about who those people are. What might be keeping them from being with us? What troubles might be part of their lives? Think of the power of good it would start for us to mention them by name and then to ask Heavenly Father to help us that we might know how to help them. Following up on such a prayer, we could do some building things.

Remember that people sheared during difficult times struggle with the added burden of cold. We need to wrap an arm of understanding around them. The extra layer of love and acceptance will add a welcome glow. The Lord gave us the charge to "strengthen your brethren in all your conversation, in all your prayers, in all your exhortations, and in all your doings" (D&C 108:7).

Paul understood this great truth and taught the Galatians: "Brethren, if a man be overtaken in a fault, ye which are spiritual, restore such an one in the spirit of meekness; considering thyself, lest thou also be tempted. Bear ye one another's burdens, and so fulfil the law of Christ." (Galatians 6:1–2.)

Paul understood because the Savior had shown him a perfect example of love. Jesus' work was to build, as was his Father's. The following is one of many examples:

> Jesus went unto the mount of Olives.
>
> And early in the morning he came again into the temple, and all the people came unto him; and he sat down, and taught them.
>
> And the scribes and Pharisees brought unto him a woman taken in adultery; and when they had set her in the midst,
>
> They say unto him, Master, this woman was taken in adultery, in the very act.
>
> Now Moses in the law commanded us, that such should be stoned: but what sayest thou?
>
> This they said, tempting him, that they might have to accuse him. But Jesus stooped down, and with his finger wrote on the ground, as though he heard them not.
>
> So when they continued asking him, he lifted up himself, and said unto them, He that is without sin among you, let him first cast a stone at her.
>
> And again he stooped down, and wrote on the ground.
>
> And they which heard it, being convicted by their own conscience, went out one by one, beginning at the eldest, even unto the last: and Jesus was left alone, and the woman standing in the midst.
>
> When Jesus had lifted up himself, and saw none but the woman, he said unto her, Woman, where are those thine accusers? hath no man condemned thee?

She said, No man, Lord. And Jesus said unto her, Neither do I condemn thee: go, and sin no more. (John 8:1–11.)

Those scribes and Pharisees seemed to keep their shears sharp and ready for use. Jesus chose to not join in their work of destruction. Instead he offered warmth and understanding while teaching a lesson for others to ponder. A cold wind of disapproval would not have helped someone who surely already knew her own faults. The Lord wrapped the woman in a warm cloak of hope. She could change. She could be forgiven.

Jesus was practicing what he had already taught when he said: "Be ye therefore merciful, as your Father also is merciful. Judge not, and ye shall not be judged: condemn not, and ye shall not be condemned: forgive, and ye shall be forgiven." (Luke 6:36–37.)

As we look to build and help others, we should remember there are many different ways we can be of service to them. Let's consider what we call the three do's of service.

1. DOING

The first of the three do's of service is simply doing things for people. It seems easy enough but can be complicated. What if our doing backfires into a shearing? It is important, therefore, that we make a righteous decision.

Alma counseled his son Corianton: "Therefore, my son, see that you are merciful unto your brethren; deal justly, judge righteously, and do good continually; and if ye do all these things then shall ye receive your reward" (Alma 41:14).

One way we can be merciful unto those who need our help would be to listen to the Spirit before we act. An illustration of this principle is found in the experience of a young lady who tried to help one of her high school classmates.

Sherry was a cheerleader and very popular with her classmates.

At the beginning of her senior year, she noticed a girl in her English class who appeared to come from poor circumstances. During the first month of school, Sherry wore all of her new back-to-school clothes but noticed that the less-fortunate girl had worn only two outfits. Sherry had been blessed with a compassionate heart, and the more she thought about her classmate the more she wanted to help her.

One evening while looking through her closet, Sherry had an idea. There were several lovely outfits that hadn't been taken out of the closet during the past year. She spent the evening cleaning the excess clothing out of her closet and putting it all in a box. The next day, full of anticipatory excitement for her service project, Sherry took the box of clothes to school and gave them to the girl in her English class. She waited for the happy shout, but immediately she knew she had made a mistake as tears of humiliation trickled quietly down the girl's cheek. Sherry's intended act of love had flipped into an act of humiliation. Sherry had never experienced hard times, and her lack of empathy impaired her helping judgment. The words of the Savior, "Judge not according to the appearance, but judge righteous judgment" (John 7:24), took on a deeper meaning.

In contrast, let's consider the actions of an elderly lady riding a bus when a young man who is crippled struggles up the entrance steps. There are no empty seats on the bus, and to her surprise and disgust no one offers to stand so that he might have a seat. The woman wants to offer her seat to the young man. But she realizes how embarrassed a young man would feel having an elderly lady give up her seat so he could sit down. Contemplating this, the woman decides instead to get off at the next stop and walk home. As she stands to get off the bus, she offers the young man her seat.

Doing service needs to be coupled with the spirit of love and compassion. If we don't know what to do, we should ask the Lord.

2. NOT DOING

One of the hardest kinds of service is that of not doing things for someone. Parents quickly learn this principle. A child whose shoes are always tied for him never learns how to tie his shoes. A child who is always reminded to take her homework back to school and has it brought to school if she forgets it never remembers on her own.

Mary tells how her twenty-two-year-old daughter Tiffany began to do things that were very destructive to herself and to the rest of the family. Mary struggled with the problems until her ideas and patience were spent. Her efforts were obviously fruitless. She was doing all of the trying, and Tiffany was enjoying her freedom. Tiffany lived at home. All of her cost-of-living bills were paid. This enabled her to spend her money on frivolous living.

Finally one day Mary told Tiffany that the free ride was over. She gave her a reasonable amount of time to move, then packed Tiffany's bags and put them out on her porch. Locking the door that evening, Mary knew the immediate encounter wouldn't be pleasant. But she was looking for more important long-range results. It was the hardest decision she had ever made.

Those results came. Not quickly. Months went by with a furious Tiffany blaming her mother for her problems. Then the growth came. And Mary's problem-daughter grew into a capable adult who thanked her mother for not doing things she needed to learn to do on her own.

We must always remember that some of the greatest service we can render in helping others may be by not doing something for them. Listening to the promptings of the Spirit will help us to make a righteous decision.

3. BEING DONE UNTO

A frequently overlooked aspect of service, especially by those who are used to being the giver, is the fact that there needs to be a receiver. That person is also giving service.

Bishop Hansen had spent a great deal of time encouraging the ward members to look for ways to fellowship new and less-active members of the ward. He felt a great responsibility to follow his own counsel.

When Kyle and his family moved in across the street, the bishop went straight over and introduced himself. He was surprised to receive a cold shoulder in response. Kyle was obviously not interested in friendship.

When Kyle's membership records showed up the following month, Bishop Hansen knew he had to try again. But adding the Church angle only increased the ice. Kyle was simply not interested. As the months went on, Bishop Hansen regularly offered and Kyle regularly refused his help.

One day he tried something new. The bishop had a cattle rack on the back of his pickup. He and his son removed the rack from the truck. Then he went over to Kyle's and asked if Kyle could help him put the rack on his truck. Kyle said he would be glad to. Several more times Kyle was asked to help in other ways. Their friendship grew and eventually flourished.

Bishop Hansen understood well the principle that some of the greatest help we can give others is by letting them do something for us. For some of us, that part of service is the most difficult. But, as Bishop Hansen discovered, this sometimes is the very key to building relationships.

Speaking of our day and time, President Gordon B. Hinckley said that for Latter-day Saints "it is a season to reach out with kindness and love to those in distress and to those who are wandering in darkness and pain. It is a time to be considerate and good, decent and courteous toward one another in all of our relationships. In other words, to become more Christlike." ("This Is the Work of the Master," *Ensign*, May 1995, p. 71.)

This can best be accomplished by heeding the whisperings of the Spirit as it lets us know when to do something, not do something, or to let someone do something for us.

School thy feelings; condemnation
Never pass on friend or foe,
Though the tide of accusation
Like a flood of truth may flow.
Hear defense before deciding,
And a ray of light may gleam,
Showing thee what filth is hiding
Underneath the shallow stream.

—*Charles W. Penrose*

7
Running the Bases

A FEW YEARS AGO WE DID something that advertised to the world our crazy thought patterns and at the same time taught us a valuable lesson. It was a hot Saturday afternoon. We had worked feverishly all morning doing the typical Saturday things, and we were tired. Going to our local department store with a whole list of purchases, we wanted our regular parking spot next to the front door, much like the designated family seat in church. But someone was in our spot! We were a bit miffed, but with disappointed sighs we made a complete swing through the parking lot and came right back to the front of the store. We saw no empty parking stalls, so we took another spin through the parking lot, with the same futile results. A few more passes, and finally we saw our foolishness. Looking around to make sure no one else had seen us emptying our gas tank to save a few steps, we sheepishly parked in the empty space at the back of the parking lot and chuckled as we made our entrance five minutes later than immediately parking and walking would have allowed us.

We blame our mind-set partly on our modern society. The hardest part of doing the dishes is clearing off the table; the hardest part of washing clothes is gathering and sorting them. We are blessed with so many great time-saving devices that we are always looking for quicker, faster ways to get things done. There are many benefits, but with that mind-set we have lost sight of the benefit that comes when we persist at something. If it isn't easy and can't be solved quickly, why would we want to do it?

There is a rule in baseball that teaches us a great application of this principle. To score in baseball, you must run around and touch all of the bases. You must go to first and then second and then third before going home. After you have touched all of the bases, then you can score. If a person were to run partway to first base and then turn around and run home, he would be out. The same is true if he went all the way to first and then straight back home. He is out! The same is true if he were to run partway to second or all the way to second or partway to third and then home. He is out!

In our relationships with others, we may have let our quicker, easier attitude affect how we deal with each other. As others step up to home plate, we size them up and lob our first pitch of conversation. Do they use the same stance at bat as we have been taught? Do they hold the bat correctly? Do they look like they belong on our team? If any of these questions are answered in the negative, why would we want to let them get to first base? Our judgment would dictate that too much time would be lost with this player. We'd keep looking for someone with the same training, with high RBIs, and that looked like he or she could belong.

In our search for the championship team, we will never score in our relationships with others. We must be willing to let them bat, and if need be we will be the pinch runner. In our quest for understanding and appreciation of others, we need to be willing to touch all of the bases. When we get up to bat, we must be patient and wait for the right pitch. Once on first we must be patient and wait to be advanced to second. If we get out before getting to third or home, we must be willing to get back up and run the bases again. We stop scoring only when we no longer are willing to get up to the plate and try getting on first. And we must never forget that we must touch all of the bases before we can score. If we don't, we will always be out!

Our relationships with each other may have been affected dramatically by our lack of patience when dealing with each other. We want to shortcut those very things that will help us build strong, loving relationships. We have all had the experience of meeting a kindred spirit, the kind we feel we knew in the premortal life. The person thinks the way we do, sees things the way we do. We want to spend time with him or her to expand that relationship.

On the other hand, we have all had the experience of meeting a porcupine person. They shoot quills at us every chance they get. We would be perfectly content to never see them again. The problem with porcupines is that they tend to hang around us for the rest of our lives. Our wish to never see them again will not be granted. They might be or become part of our family, live in our neighborhood, or be part of our work or Church experience. Now what? When porcupines are part of our life, we have two choices. Either they can be a constant irritant to us, or we can take the time to understand their secrets and know who they really are and learn to accept them and love them as a true brother or sister. This will take going around and touching all the bases.

"But," we may whine, "he's a porcupine! He's not like we are!"

One of the beautiful things about us is that no two of us are exactly alike. Even identical twins are different. Elder Francis M. Gibbons of the Seventy described this as follows:

> We are all alike, and yet so very different. This truth reflects one of the most unusual aspects of the Creation, that there should be such wide diversity in the midst of apparent uniformity. . . .
>
> We learn, for example, that there are no two sets of fingerprints exactly alike. Thus, of the billions of people who have lived, who now live, or who may yet live, each has a special identifying mark at the tips of his fingers. . . .
>
> And, we are told, each of us who writes has a different style from all others. Our voices are different, too. The differences in

timbre, in tone, in volume, in inflection, in cadence, all make it possible for us to identify someone on the telephone without ever having heard the name mentioned. But again, these and other physical differences not visible to the eye still do not tell the full story, for there is within each of us a spirit that preexisted earth life, that stands apart from all others. ("One Out of Many," *Brigham Young University 1990–91 Devotional and Fireside Speeches* [Provo, Utah: University Publications, 1991], pp. 33–34.)

In light of this truth, it would seem futile for us to reject those who are not like us, for no two people are exactly alike. To the obvious physical differences we could add the fact that none of us have had the same experience in this life. Each life lived is unique. So many times we judge ourselves and others by using comparison. That is a Satan-inspired part of our society. It begins with our children as babies: "How big was your baby? Only nine pounds, eight ounces? My oldest was eleven pounds." "Is your baby walking yet? My little Jared started to walk three months ago! I know that's early, but he's done everything early." "Does Suzy know her colors yet? Sarah learned hers at a special preschool we've enrolled her in. We didn't want her to get behind even before kindergarten." Then comes the sports teams: who wins, who loses, who is the outstanding player. And school—who spelled the best, who ran the fastest in PE, who got the best grades. Is it any wonder that we as adults use comparison as our worthiness barometer?

The fallacy with this thinking is that the one who will judge us doesn't compare us with anyone. He will never look at our neighbor and say, "You're right, John isn't as good as Jerry." Then how does he judge us?

"For I, the Lord, will judge all men according to their works, according to the desire of their hearts" (D&C 137:9). "For of him unto whom much is given much is required; and he who sins against the greater light shall receive the greater condemnation" (D&C 82:3).

In other words, we are judged by what we do with what we are given. No comparisons. No contests. Are we headed in the right direction? Are we doing better today than we did yesterday? Are we a better person this year than last year?

When we throw comparisons out the window and understand the truth that no two people are exactly alike, we eliminate a lot of wasted time and energy. That time would be more productively spent trying to learn from others and trying to understand them better. When we stop expecting others to be like us and spend more time learning to accept others as they are, our love for others will grow.

As others step up to the plate, what should we look for? Are they good-looking, rich, famous, or perfect? That's the worldly, satanic scope and is counter to what Heavenly Father has provided for us through the Savior's mission. There is only one initial mind-set we should see when they step up to the base: that they are an infinitely loved child of our Father in Heaven.

Our habit may be to see what might stand out the most as they step up to home plate. That might be a big personality flaw, tattered clothes, or a dark countenance. The Lord has asked us to focus on the good and to build. He counseled: "And why beholdest thou the mote that is in thy brother's eye, but considerest not the beam that is in thine own eye? Or how wilt thou say to thy brother, Let me pull out the mote out of thine eye; and, behold, a beam is in thine own eye?" (Matthew 7:3–4.) Satan knows that we as humans can focus only on one thing at a time. If he can get us to focus on the faults of others, it will distract us from overcoming our own shortcomings. We can all learn from the following statement of Thomas B. Marsh, who was at one time the President of the Quorum of the Twelve Apostles. He was excommunicated from the Church on March 17, 1839. When he rejoined the Church in July 1857 he made this observation:

I have sought diligently to know the Spirit of Christ since I turned my face Zionward, and I believe I have obtained it. I have frequently wanted to know how my apostacy began, and I have come to the conclusion that I must have lost the Spirit of the Lord out of my heart.

The next question is, "How and when did you lose the Spirit?" I became jealous of the Prophet, and then I saw double, and overlooked everything that was right, and spent all my time in looking for the evil; and then, when the Devil began to lead me, it was easy for the carnal mind to rise up, which is anger, jealousy, and wrath. I could feel it within me; I felt angry and wrathful; and the Spirit of the Lord being gone, as the Scriptures say, I was blinded, and I thought I saw a beam in brother Joseph's eye, but it was nothing but a mote, and my own eye was filled with the beam; but I thought I saw a beam in his, and I wanted to get it out; and, as brother Heber says, I got mad, and I wanted everybody else to be mad. I talked with Brother Brigham and Brother Heber, and I wanted them to be mad like myself; and I saw they were not mad, and I got madder still because they were not. Brother Brigham, with a cautious look, said, "Are you the leader of the Church, brother Thomas?" I answered, "No." "Well then," said he, "Why do you not let that alone?" (In *Journal of Discourses*, 5:206–7.)

Thomas B. Marsh's focus was in the wrong direction, much like a historian that Elder Boyd K. Packer of the Quorum of the Twelve Apostles described:

Some time ago a historian gave a lecture to an audience of college students on one of the past Presidents of the Church. It seemed to be his purpose to show that that President was a man subject to the foibles of men. He introduced many so-called facts that put that President in a very unfavorable light, particularly when they were taken out of the context of the historical period in which he lived. . . .

What that historian did with the reputation of the President of the Church was not worth doing. He seemed determined to convince everyone that the *prophet* was a *man*. We knew that already. All of the prophets and all of the Apostles have been men. It would have been much more worthwhile for him to convince us that the *man* was a *prophet*, a fact quite as true as the fact that he was a man. (*Let Not Your Heart Be Troubled* [Salt Lake City: Bookcraft, 1991], pp. 106–7, 108.)

Joseph Smith the Prophet had some words to say on this subject: "I will give you one of the *Keys* of the mysteries of the Kingdom. It is an eternal principle, that has existed with God from all eternity: That man who rises up to condemn others, finding fault with the Church, saying that they are out of the way, while he himself is righteous, then know assuredly, that that man is in the high road to apostasy; and if he does not repent, will apostatize, as God lives." (*The Teachings of Joseph Smith*, eds. Larry E. Dahl and Donald Q. Cannon [Salt Lake City: Bookcraft, 1997], p. 43.)

Look for the positive. Above all, remember the secrets. Be patient with others, keeping in mind that you don't know all of their secrets. One of the most important secrets that you don't know is their level of understanding of gospel principles. The Lord distinguishes between follies and sins, as he taught us in the Doctrine and Covenants.

In 1836 the Saints and their leaders were facing a challenging situation. Among other things, the Church had a sizeable debt; many members were moving into the Kirtland, Ohio, area, some of whom were in need of financial assistance; money was needed for various land purchases; and hard currency was scarce. Finding ways to address these challenges was an important priority for Church leaders. The book *Church History in the Fulness of Times* (The Church of Jesus Christ of Latter-day Saints, 1989) describes what happened at this time:

In July of 1836 a Brother Burgess arrived in Kirtland and told Joseph Smith that he knew where a large sum of money was hidden in the cellar of a certain house in Salem, Massachusetts. He claimed to be the only person living who knew of the treasure and the location of the house. Salem was a prosperous seaport with a world trade, so it was plausible that treasure would be located there. Hunting for buried treasure, especially that left by Spanish pirates, was still widespread among Americans in that area. Persuaded by Burgess, the Prophet, with Sidney Rigdon, Hyrum Smith, and Oliver Cowdery, left Kirtland in late July. . . .

. . . Even with the help of Burgess, the brethren searched in vain for the house with the supposed treasure. Burgess soon departed, explaining that Salem had changed so much since he was last there that he could not find the house. (P. 170.)

While the brethren were in Salem, the Lord gave the Prophet a revelation, the first part of which reads: "I, the Lord your God, am not displeased with your coming this journey, notwithstanding your follies" (D&C 111:1).

They hadn't sinned. They had done something using their own wisdom and experience. It wasn't the smartest thing they could have done, but it wasn't a sin.

That's the way a folly is, someone doing the best they can according to their knowledge and background. It may be different than what our knowledge and background would have us do. Patience to wait for growth and learning is part of running the bases.

In our quest to develop strong personal relationships, we may get weary as we make our path from home to first, home to second. Our patience may wear thin. When we're tempted to give up, we need to remember a beautiful scripture found in 1 Nephi 21:15–16: "For can a woman forget her sucking child, that she should not have compassion on the son of her womb? Yea, they may forget, yet will I not forget thee, O house of Israel. Behold, I have graven thee upon the palms of my hands; thy walls are continually before me."

Those of us who have nursed babies know how difficult it is to forget that baby. When the breakfast milk is made, the mother will become engorged and miserable if the baby doesn't drink it until dinner. By that time, lunch and dinner milk has also been made.

The Savior says it would be harder for him to forget us than for the mother to forget her child. He remembers Gethsemane and Calvary. He has graven that memory upon the palms of his hands.

Then he says, "Thy walls are continually before me." Though the term *walls* in the original context of this scripture may have to do with the restoration of the house of Israel, we might think of it here as referring to personal walls or barriers. What do walls do? They stop us from going forward. They block our progress. He knows the secret that is causing the wall. He knows the difficult circumstances brick by brick that compose our individual walls. He has watched and felt every brick. Some of us have knee-high walls that others can step over. Unfortunately, some have walls that are high and seemingly impenetrable.

These fortresses are always before the Savior. He knows each brick and knows which of those bricks are loose. Everyone has at least one loose brick. That loose brick might be a hobby, a baby, a death, or an illness. Every home or visiting teacher, bishop, neighbor, and friend who relies on the promptings of the Spirit will be directed in the removal of the first brick. Each succeeding brick will come out easier after that first brick is removed. It just takes time and patience.

A scripture in Alma talks about nourishing the word. Substituting *relationships* for *the word* says exactly how it works: "But if ye will nourish *relationships*, yea, nourish the tree as it beginneth to grow, by your faith with great diligence, and with patience, looking forward to the fruit thereof, it shall take root; and behold it shall be a tree springing up unto everlasting life. And because of your diligence and your faith and your patience with the *relationship* in nourishing it, that it may take root in you, behold, by and by ye shall pluck the fruit thereof, which is most precious. . . . Then, my brethren, ye shall reap the rewards of your faith, and your diligence, and patience, and long-suffering, waiting for the tree to bring forth fruit unto you." (Alma 32:41–43.)

Running all the bases will bring us treasured friendships.

He is our Heavenly Father; he is also our God, and the Maker and upholder of all things in heaven and on earth. He sends forth his counsels and extends his providences to all living. He is the Supreme Controller of the universe. . . . [T]he hairs of our heads are numbered by him . . . ; and he knoweth every thought and intent of the hearts of all living, for he is everywhere present by the power of his Spirit—his minister, the Holy Ghost. He is the Father of all, is above all, through all, and in you all; he knoweth all things pertaining to this earth, and he knows all things pertaining to millions of earths like this.

—*Brigham Young*

8

Judging God

MAX HAD A GREAT DESIRE TO serve a mission. As he made the necessary preparations to receive his call, he had a strong impression that he would serve a mission in the Far East, specifically Taiwan. Over the next several weeks, the impression grew into a burning desire, and by the time he had his interview with his stake president, he was more than ready. The custom at that time was for the stake president to ask if the missionary had any preference where he would like to serve. When the big question was finally asked, Max quickly answered, "The Far East, Taiwan." The stake president nodded his approval, filled in the appropriate box, and put the papers in an envelope bound for Church headquarters.

Max expectantly watched the mailbox until the call finally arrived. He fingered the envelope, savoring the excitement for a moment before he opened the call. *Taiwan, here I come,* he thought as he unfolded the letter, which read: "You are hereby called to be a missionary of The Church of Jesus Christ of Latter-day Saints to labor in the California Mission." California! He read it again. Excitement quickly gave way to confusion. Inspiration? Taiwan? Wow. He was heading clear to California.

There are some prayers that are mundane and repetitive. But the prayer he prayed that night was a fervent plea for an understanding of what appeared to him to be an erroneous call. His prayer was answered as the Holy Ghost quietly filled his soul with the assurance that God knew what he was doing and that yes, indeed, he was to serve a mission in California. Why? He wasn't told. He knew for certain only that it was God's will.

Many of us have had times like Max's when we question God. Sometimes we pray for something that doesn't happen or for something not to happen and it does. We may wonder if God has really listened. Is he really aware of what is going on? We may judge God. Many times we eventually find out how foolish we have been. Such was the case with Max and his call to serve in California.

Max had a wonderful mission. He taught people he felt had been especially prepared to receive the gospel message through him. One family of five particularly highlighted his California mission experience. They had been taught by several sets of missionaries with no success. Max and his companion followed up when they were assigned to the area. There was an immediate bond. Max and the family seemed to have an extraordinary link. Within a few weeks, the entire family was committed to baptism. The day they were baptized confirmed Max's feelings. He was serving where he was supposed to serve.

Max and the family continued their special link even after he returned home from his mission. Years passed. He and the family continued to keep in touch through Christmas letters. One special letter contained the news that their son had been called to serve a mission to Taiwan. Taiwan! Max finally understood. His California mission had planted the seed that blossomed into a mission to Taiwan.

Heavenly Father has perfect vision. We should never try to judge his wisdom through our myopic judgment. If we give him time to work his wonders, we will inevitably know the wisdom of his decisions. It will take faith, confidence, and, most important of all, humility to realize that God knows better than we do what is best.

A story from an old Arab legend can help us understand God's panoramic view.

The great prophet Moses was visited by angels and invited to come to heaven. While there he noticed God giving orders to some of his angels. Curious, Moses asked if he could accompany an angel on his mission. The Lord was reluctant at first to send Moses, claiming that he would not be able to understand what the angels had been sent to do, but with further pleading he finally consented, with a condition. Moses must promise not to question the things he would see. To this Moses agreed and soon found himself flying with the angel down to earth.

They first flew over the water until they came to a small fishing boat upon which seven poor fishermen were trying to catch their daily sustenance. As they flew nearer, the angel looked upon them and waved his arm. Immediately the ship broke in half and all seven of the humble fishermen drowned. Moses was stunned at this and began questioning the angel. The angel reprimanded Moses, reminding him of his promise, and they flew on in silence.

The second circumstance found them flying over the desert near a small village. Walking down a dusty path was a young boy of about ten. As they flew by, the angel once again waved his arm and the young boy dropped dead on the path. Moses was again astonished at the irrational behavior of the angel and began to protest loudly until the angel again silenced him by reminding him of his promise to the Lord. A quiet but angry Moses continued the journey with the angel, confused that the Lord would send an angel to work such destruction and sorrow upon innocent people.

The third episode involved a small family living on the outskirts of a large city. Along the caravan road entering the city lived a poor widow and her only son. They were desperately poor and lived solely upon the meager harvest of a small garden scratched into the dust of their backyard. The garden was alongside an old stone wall erected to separate the home from the caravan route into the city. As Moses and the angel flew by, he once again waved his arm, and the stone fence fell into the widow's garden, destroying all the produce. At this unexpected turn of events, Moses could no longer be silent in his protesting and the angel took him back to heaven and to the Lord.

Moses asked the Lord why he would do such things, and the Lord reminded him of the warning that he would not be able to understand the workings of God. After further protests, the Lord decided the only way to teach Moses would be to send him again with the angel, this time to see things he had not seen before.

Once again Moses and the angel flew over the water where the fishermen had perished. Debris and wreckage still floated on the surface of the water. As Moses watched, he saw something that he could not see the first time. Far over the horizon, just barely in view, he noticed another boat. The angel allowed Moses to see what would have been had he not been sent of God. The other boat was full of pirates, and Moses knew that the fishermen would have been captured, tortured, and sold into slavery had the Lord not in his mercy chosen to bring them home.

They then passed the young Arab, still lifeless along the desert path. Moses was allowed to see that later that same afternoon this young boy would have accidentally killed his brother. According to the custom of the village, he would have been disowned by his family and made an outcast in the town, being forced to make his living begging in the streets until death from disease freed him from his misery.

Finally, they flew over the widow's garden, where the woman and her son were struggling to salvage something from the chaos that was once their garden. As the young boy dug away the earth under a large rock, he noticed a small cache. Investigating further he found a small chest. He called to his mother, and they looked inside and found a treasure trove of jewels and riches enough to provide a comfortable living for them for the remainder of their lives.

With a smile, Moses flew back to heaven with the angel. He finally understood what the Lord had been trying to tell him.

As we consider this legend, the words of Isaiah come to mind: "For my thoughts are not your thoughts, neither are your ways my ways, saith the Lord. For as the heavens are higher than the earth, so are my ways higher than your ways, and my thoughts than your thoughts." (Isaiah 55:8–9.)

The most common error made when we judge the things God does is that we assume we know why he has done it. The story is told of a man who was asleep one night, when he suddenly found his room filled with light. The Lord appeared to him and told him he had a work for him to do. He showed the man a large rock, explaining that he was to push the rock with all his might. The man went and did as he was instructed. Day after day he pushed against the rock with all of his strength. Each day the man came home worn out and very discouraged because he felt that his whole day had been spent in vain. Satan took advantage of these feelings and tried to convince the man that he was wasting his time on an impossible task. Satan's attempt to dishearten the efforts of this dutiful servant began to have an effect on his attitude. He now wondered if the job he had been asked to do was possible. He wondered what was wrong with him and why the Lord was not helping him move the rock. In this moment of futility he turned to the Lord for answers. The Lord's explanation to the man contains a message we should never forget. The Lord acknowledged that the man had done exactly as he had been commanded. He had faithfully pushed against the rock every day. With an understanding smile, the Lord pointed out that he had never said he wanted the rock moved. The man had falsely assumed that moving the rock was part of the request. Working feverishly to accomplish his mistaken goal left him frustrated at his apparent wasted time and effort.

With new understanding, the man listened as he was taught the real mission of the rock. The Lord had him look at his newly acquired muscles gained from pushing against that massive weight.

The opposition had made his muscles strong. And his faith and obedience had strengthened his spiritual self as well. His time and energy had been well worth his newly acquired strength.

Another example of our erroneous judgment of the things God commands can be found in our perceived knowledge of the Word of Wisdom. The Lord commanded us not to drink coffee. We have assumed the ban on coffee is because of the high level of caffeine. The Lord never stated the reason. He asked us not to drink it because it is not good for us. We all know that caffeine regularly consumed in high doses is not good for us and that coffee has caffeine in it. However, as recent studies have shown, coffee contains other hidden harmful substances.

We must learn to have faith in God's commands and try not to second-guess his reasons for giving the command. If we faithfully follow his directives, we will eventually know his mind concerning the matter. In John we read: "If any man will do his will, he shall know of the doctrine, whether it be of God, or whether I speak of myself" (7:17). It is not that we should never try to figure out why God has asked us to do something, but if that effort becomes a stumbling block to our obedience to the command, then we are robbing ourselves of great knowledge of the things of God.

A solider during the Vietnam War was captured by the enemy and put in a prisoner-of-war camp. The conditions were terrible, and he could see no immediate hope of being rescued from the ever-growing hours of terror. He started praying, asking God why this had happened to him. The more he prayed, the more frustrated he became as the heavens seemed closed to his pleas. After months of petitioning the Lord, he finally received a simple response: "You're asking the wrong question." Pondering the answer, the man came to realize that instead of asking why this was happening to him he needed to ask what he was to learn from all of this suffering. He immediately changed his prayer to "Please teach me what thou wantest me to learn." His dreadful ordeal lasted seven years. Each day of his imprisonment was begun with the same prayerful inquiry, "What can this day teach me?" His correct questioning was daily rewarded by insightful answers. Seven years of potentially wasted imprisonment became years of great growth and understanding.

Our myopic vision about God's answers are not the only way that we err. God reveals his knowledge and desires to his servants in wards and stakes throughout the worldwide Church, and that secondary voice is sometimes misjudged too. It's obvious to those who believe in divine inspiration that misjudging his servants is misjudging God. The Lord himself stated: "What I the Lord have spoken, I have spoken, and I excuse not myself; and though the heavens and the earth pass away, my word shall not pass away, but shall all be fulfilled, whether by mine own voice or by the voice of my servants, it is the same" (D&C 1:38).

Because the Lord's servants are human, we sometimes find fault with them and with what they say. This is not only wrong but can be fatal spiritually. The Lord counseled us concerning this: "And the arm of the Lord shall be revealed; and the day cometh that they who will not hear the voice of the Lord, neither the voice of his servants, neither give heed to the words of the prophets and apostles, shall be cut off from among the people" (D&C 1:14).

When the Lord's chosen servants speak, we must not try to outguess what the Lord is teaching or think that our way is better. As soon as we do, we are in serious jeopardy of losing our eternal salvation. As pointed out in a previous chapter, the Prophet Joseph Smith taught: "That man who rises up to condemn others, finding fault with the Church, saying that they are out of the way, while he himself is righteous, then know assuredly, that that man is in the high road to apostasy; and if he does not repent, will apostatize, as God lives" (*The Teachings of Joseph Smith*, eds. Larry E. Dahl and Donald Q. Cannon [Salt Lake City: Bookcraft, 1997], p. 43).

If we have the faith and patience to follow the Lord's servants when they speak his will and put our opinions aside, greater knowledge and understanding will come to us. Elder M. Russell Ballard of the Quorum of the Twelve Apostles related the following:

> President David O. McKay told of a meeting of the Council of the Twelve Apostles where a question of grave importance was discussed. He and the other Apostles felt strongly about a certain course of action that should be taken, and they were prepared to share their feelings in a meeting with the First Presidency. To their surprise, President Joseph F. Smith did not ask for their opinion in the matter, as was his custom. Rather, "he arose and said, 'This is what the Lord wants.'
>
> "While it was not wholly in harmony with what he had decided . . . ," President McKay wrote, "the President of the Twelve . . . was the first on his feet to say, 'Brethren, I move that that becomes the opinion and judgment of this Council.'
>
> " 'Second the motion,' said another, and it was unanimous. Six months did not pass before the wisdom of that leader was demonstrated" (*Gospel Ideals*, Salt Lake City: *Improvement Era*, 1953, p. 264). ("Strength in Counsel," *Ensign*, November 1993, p. 78.)

The true test of our faith in this life is to put all faith in God and his word. God will always be vindicated. The world may mock and profess a better way, but rest assured that God's direction is the right direction which will lead us to eternal life.

What is our response when we are offended, misunderstood, unfairly or unkindly treated . . . ? Do we resent, become bitter, hold a grudge? Or do we resolve the problem if we can, forgive, and rid ourselves of the burden?

The nature of our response to such situations may well determine the nature and quality of our lives, here and eternally.

—*Marion D. Hanks*

9

The Forgiving Heart

WE ALL HAVE SECRETS THAT prompt us to act in a certain way. Our neighbors, our families, and our acquaintances all have secrets that prompt them to act in a certain way. We all react differently to different situations. Is it any wonder that these secrets sometimes cause actions that bump one another?

The experience is universal. It is impossible for us to go through life without having someone bump our feelings. Sometimes the bump is only a nudge, without any lasting effects. Other bumps can cause bruising that goes away with time. But sometimes the bump is a head-on collision that leaves devastating ramifications. Life's experiences might put us directly in the collision. Even more difficult might be our involvement in a chain reaction reverberating from a collision involving someone we love. Our feelings are hurt. We hurt for them. A bitter seed is planted. Now what? Should we get even? Should we forgive?

The Savior taught the Apostles about forgiveness. In those days, the rabbis said that no one was under obligation to forgive a neighbor more than three times. Peter, asking the Savior for a ruling on the matter, reasoned that if a person forgave seven times, that would be a great improvement. But seven times fell short of the celestial law that would govern those who followed the Master. The Lord said, "Until seventy times seven" (Matthew 18:22).

That number means we need to forgive, and forgive, and forgive. The number is practically an unlimited amount of times. When we choose to follow the Savior, we choose to obey the celestial law of forgiveness number one: always forgive.

The celestial law of forgiveness number two tells us whom we have to forgive: "I, the Lord, will forgive whom I will forgive, but of you it is required to forgive all men" (D&C 64:10). When we put the two celestial laws of forgiveness together, they can simply be stated in four words: Always forgive all people.

Obviously, we're not all ready to live the entire celestial law. We need to remember that becoming perfect is a process, not an event. The Christian writer C. S. Lewis perceived this concept: "It may be hard for an egg to turn into a bird: it would be a jolly sight harder for it to learn to fly while remaining an egg. We are like eggs at present. And you cannot go on indefinitely being just an ordinary, decent egg. We must be hatched or go bad." (*Mere Christianity* [New York: Macmillan, 1952; Collier Books, 1960], p. 169.)

Those four simple words—always forgive all people—form a strong shell, making hatching difficult for those who have been hit with a head-on offense. Harder still for most of us is forgiveness when someone we love has been offended or hurt. This you-can-mess-with-me-but-don't-mess-with-my-spouse-or-my-kids attitude puts a whole new wrinkle in the forgiveness problem. But the command remains the same: forgive everyone every time. Those rules cancel out every "but what if?" Perhaps it will help us to move forward if we understand the reasons we should forgive.

We know that no unclean thing can dwell in the presence of God (see Moses 6:57). And we are painfully aware of Paul's statement that "all have sinned, and come short of the glory of God" (Romans 3:23). Obviously, we are all going to make mistakes and add up a sizable amount of sins in our sojourn on earth. We will need forgiveness. But forgiveness of others is a condition for obtaining forgiveness for ourselves: "For if ye forgive men their trespasses, your heavenly Father will also forgive you: but if ye forgive not men their trespasses, neither will your Father forgive your trespasses" (Matthew 6:14–15).

Now, there's a good, straightforward reason to forgive. Upon the conditions of repentance and of forgiveness of others, we can have our own sins forgiven and paid for by the Redeemer.

There is another reason, one that will affect us both now and eternally. Its effects spread to others and can trickle down through our posterity. The following story told by Elder John H. Groberg of the Seventy is a fine example:

In the early 1900s, a young father and his family joined the Church in Hawaii. He was enthused about his new-found religion, and after two years of membership both he and his eldest son held the priesthood. They prospered and enjoyed the fellowship of the little branch. They anxiously looked forward to being sealed as a family for eternity in the temple soon to be completed in Laie.

Then, as so often happens, a test crossed their path. One of their daughters became ill with an unknown disease and was taken away to a strange hospital. People in Hawaii were understandably wary of unknown diseases, as such diseases had wrought so much havoc there.

The concerned family went to church the next Sunday, looking forward to the strength and understanding they would receive from their fellow members. It was a small branch. This young father and his son very often took the responsibility for blessing and passing the sacrament. This was one such Sunday. They reverently broke the bread while the congregation sang the sacrament hymn. When the hymn was finished, the young father began to kneel to offer the sacrament prayer. Suddenly the branch president, realizing who was at the sacred table, sprang to his feet. He pointed his finger and cried, "Stop. You can't touch the sacrament. Your daughter has an unknown disease. Leave immediately while someone else fixes new sacrament bread. We can't have you here. Go."

How would you react? What would you do?

The stunned father slowly stood up. He searchingly looked at the branch president, then at the congregation. Then, sensing the depth of anxiety and embarrassment from all, he motioned to his family and they quietly filed out of the chapel.

Not a word was said as, with faces to the ground, they moved along the dusty trail to their small home. The young son noticed the firmness in his father's clenched fists and the tenseness of his set jaw. When they entered their home they all sat in a circle, and the father said, "We will be silent until I am ready to speak." All sorts of thoughts went through the mind of this young boy. He envisioned his father coming up with many novel ways of getting revenge. Would they kill the branch president's pigs, or burn his house, or join another church? He could hardly wait to see what would happen.

Five minutes, ten minutes, fifteen minutes—not a sound. He glanced at his father. His eyes were closed, his mouth was set, his fingers clenched, but no sound. Twenty minutes, twenty-five minutes—still nothing. Then he noticed a slight relaxing of his father's hands, a small tremor on his father's lips, then a barely perceptible sob. He looked at his father—tears were trickling down his cheeks from closed eyes. Soon he noticed his mother was crying also, then one child, then another, and soon the whole family.

Finally, the father opened his eyes, cleared his throat, and announced, "I am now ready to speak. Listen carefully." He slowly turned to his wife and said, meaningfully, "I love you." Then turning to each child, he told them individually, "I love you. I love all of you and I want us to be together, forever, as a family. And the only way that can be is for all of us to be good members of The Church of Jesus Christ of Latter-day Saints and be sealed by his holy priesthood in the temple. This is not the branch president's church. It is the Church of Jesus Christ. We will not let any man or any amount of hurt or embarrassment or pride keep us from being together forever. Next Sunday we will go back to church. We will stay by ourselves until our daughter's sickness is known, but we will go back."

This great man had proper eternal perspective.

The daughter's health problem was resolved; the family did go to the temple when it was completed. The children did remain faithful and were likewise sealed to their own families in the temple as time went on. Today over 100 souls in this family are active members of the Church and call their father, grandfather, and great-grandfather blessed because he kept his eyes on eternity. ("Writing Your Personal and Family History," *Ensign*, May 1980, p. 49.)

This wonderful father made a choice to forgive. That choice affected the spiritual well-being of himself, his family, and his posterity. What does hatred do to us? Elder Orson F. Whitney of the Quorum of the Twelve Apostles said, "We are required to forgive all men, for our own sakes, since hatred retards spiritual growth" (in Rulon T. Burton, *We Believe: Doctrines and Principles of The Church of Jesus Christ of Latter-day Saints* [Salt Lake City: Tabernacle Books, 1994], p. 282). Hatred turns us away from the Spirit. This pivotal reason to forgive will affect us now and eternally. In October 1973 general conference, Elder Marion D. Hanks, then an Assistant to the Council of the Twelve, highlighted the importance of choosing to forgive:

Not only our eternal salvation depends upon our willingness and capacity to forgive wrongs committed against us. Our joy and satisfaction in this life, and our true freedom, depend upon our doing so. When Christ bade us turn the other cheek, walk the second mile, give our cloak to him who takes our coat, was it to be chiefly out of consideration for the bully, the brute, the thief? Or was it to relieve the one aggrieved of the destructive burden that resentment and anger lay upon us?

Paul wrote to the Romans that nothing "shall be able to separate us from the love of God, which is in Christ Jesus our Lord." (Rom. 8:39.)

I am sure this is true. I bear testimony that this is true. But it is also true that we can *separate ourselves* from his spirit. . . .

In every case of sin this is true. Envy, arrogance, unrighteous dominion—these canker the soul of one who is guilty of them. It is true also if we fail to forgive. Even if it appears that another may be deserving of our resentment or hatred, none of us can afford to pay the price of resenting or hating, because of what it does to us. . . .

It is reported that President Brigham Young once said that he who takes offense when no offense was intended is a fool, and he who takes offense when offense *was* intended is usually a fool. It was then explained that there are two courses of action to follow when one is bitten by a rattlesnake. One may, in anger, fear, or vengefulness, pursue the creature and kill it. Or he may make full haste to get the venom out of his system. If we pursue the latter course we will likely survive, but if we attempt to follow the former, we may not be around long enough to finish it. ("Forgiveness: The Ultimate Form of Love," *Ensign*, January 1974, pp. 20–21.)

The venom of anger and bitterness can poison us spiritually. Any form of pursuing those who have wronged us spreads that poison through our own spiritual bodies and can spread to affect the lives of others. Elder Boyd K. Packer of the Quorum of the Twelve Apostles was taught this lesson by a saintly mentor, who at the time of Elder Packer's acquaintance was a patriarch whose life had been full of sterling Church and community service:

On one occasion when we were alone and the spirit was right, he gave me a lesson for my life from an experience in his. Although I thought I had known him, he told me things I would not have supposed.

He grew up in a little community. Somehow in his youth he had a desire to make something of himself and struggled success-fully to get an education.

He married a lovely young woman, and presently everything in his life was just right. He was well employed, with a bright future. They were deeply in love, and she was expecting their first child.

The night the baby was to be born there were complications. The only doctor was somewhere in the countryside tending to the sick. They were not able to find him. After many hours of labor the condition of the mother-to-be became desperate.

Finally the doctor arrived. He sensed the emergency, acted quickly, and soon had things in order. The baby was born and the crisis, it appeared, was over.

Some days later the young mother died from the very infection that the doctor had been treating at the other home that night.

My friend's world was shattered. Everything was not right now; everything was all wrong. He had lost his wife, his sweetheart. He had no way to take care of a tiny baby and at once tend to his work.

As the weeks wore on his grief festered. "That doctor should not be allowed to practice," he would say. "He brought that infection to my wife; if he had been careful she would be alive today." He thought of little else, and in his bitterness he became threatening.

Then one night a knock came at his door. A little youngster said, simply, "Daddy wants you to come over. He wants to talk to you."

"Daddy" was the stake president. A grieving, heartbroken young man went to see his spiritual leader. This spiritual shepherd had been watching his flock and had something to say to him.

The counsel from this wise servant was simply: "John, leave it alone. Nothing you do about it will bring her back. Anything you do will make it worse. John, leave it alone."

My friend told me then that this had been his trial, his Gethse-mane.

How could he leave it alone? Right was right! A terrible wrong had been committed, and somebody must pay for it.

He struggled in agony to get hold of himself. It did not happen at once. Finally he determined that whatever else the issues were, he should be obedient.

Obedience is a powerful spiritual medicine. It comes close to being a cure-all.

He determined to follow the counsel of that wise spiritual leader. He would leave it alone.

Then he told me, "I was an old man before I finally understood. It was not until I was an old man that I could finally see a poor country doctor—overworked, underpaid, run ragged from patient to patient, with little proper medicine, no hospital, few instruments. He struggled to save lives, and succeeded for the most part.

"He had come in a moment of crisis when two lives hung in the balance and had acted without delay.

"I was an old man," he repeated, "before finally I understood. I would have ruined my life," he said, "and the lives of others."

Many times he had thanked the Lord on his knees for a wise spiritual leader who counseled simply, "John, leave it alone." (*"That All May Be Edified"* [Salt Lake City: Bookcraft, 1982], pp. 66–67.)

When Bette was growing up, Mutual was always Tuesday night at 7:30. Before the lesson or activity, the young men and young women always met in the chapel for joint opening exercises. They always had a song and prayer and then stood together to say the scripture that was the theme for the year. One year, the theme was found in Doctrine and Covenants 130:20–21: "There is a law, irrevocably decreed in heaven before the foundations of this world, upon which all blessings are predicated—and when we obtain any blessing from God, it is by obedience to that law upon which it is predicated."

The celestial law is, Always forgive all people. Obedience to that law brought John a blessing of joy he couldn't have imagined. That same lesson was learned by President Heber J. Grant when he felt the difference between the joy that follows obedience to that law and the hollow anger of an unforgiving heart.

Many years ago a prominent man was excommunicated from the Church. Years later, he pleaded for baptism. President John Taylor referred the question of his rebaptism to the Apostles, saying that the baptism was conditional upon a unanimous consent. The first vote was five for baptism and seven against.

About a year later the question was once again brought before the quorum. This time the vote was eight for baptism and four against. In the final vote, Heber J. Grant, then next to the junior member of the quorum, was the only opposing vote.

President John Taylor called him into his office and asked how he would feel when he went to the other side and found he had kept this man from entering with those who have repented of their sins and received some reward?

Heber J. Grant replied that he could look the Lord squarely in the eye and tell him that he did that which he thought was for the best good of the kingdom. The man had disgraced the Church enough, and he didn't propose to let any such man come back into the Church.

President Taylor told him he should stay with his convictions. Elder Grant went home to eat lunch. While there, he opened his Doctrine and Covenants. There was a bookmark where he had last read, but the book opened instead to: "Wherefore, I say unto you, that ye ought to forgive one another; for he that forgiveth not his brother his trespasses standeth condemned before the Lord. . . . I, the Lord, will forgive whom I will forgive, but of you it is required to forgive all men." (D&C 64:9–10.)

As he closed the book, he said, "If the devil applies for baptism, and claims that he has repented, I will baptize him."

After lunch, he returned to the office of President Taylor and told him he had a change of heart. One hour before he had thought that never while he lived did he expect to ever consent that Brother So-and-so should be baptized, but he told President Taylor that he could be baptized as far as he was concerned.

Apparently pleased, President Taylor laughed and said, "My boy, the change is very sudden, very sudden. I want to ask you a question. How did you feel when you left here an hour ago? Did you feel like you wanted to hit that man right squarely between the eyes and knock him down?"

Heber J. Grant replied that was just the way he felt.

President Taylor asked how he felt at that moment.

Elder Grant said he hoped the Lord would forgive the sinner.

The prophet said, "You feel very happy, don't you, in comparison. You had the spirit of anger, you had the spirit of bitterness in your heart toward that man, because of his sin and because of the disgrace he had brought upon the Church. And now you have the spirit of forgiveness and you really feel happy, don't you?" (See Heber J. Grant, *Gospel Standards* [Salt Lake City: *Improvement Era*, 1969], pp. 259–62.)

How could Heber J. Grant change like that? One hour had turned his heart from bitterness to joy. Can a mortal being change like that by himself? Left alone, he probably would have stayed firm in his unforgiving conviction. But the Lord used a most powerful weapon against that hatred. It's a weapon that we can draw upon if forgiving seems too hard. There are some things we can't do alone.

Jacob 4:7 says that "the Lord God showeth us our weakness that we may know that it is by his grace, and his great condescensions unto the children of men, that we have power to do these things." The great weapon we can all use is the grace of our Savior. Grace is when someone does something for us that we can't do by ourselves. We cannot rise to forgive some sins. There may be too much pain. The bitterness or hatred may have simmered too long. The secret may have been hidden in our hearts too long and too deeply for us to be able to rid ourselves of the poison. But the Savior, through his grace, can help. He invites us to use that grace and that power to rid ourselves of the heavy burden of bitterness: "Come unto me, all ye that labour and are heavy laden, and I will give you rest. Take my yoke upon you, . . . and ye shall find rest unto your souls." (Matthew 11:28–29.)

Rest, peace, and joy will be ours if we allow the Savior to put the arms of his yoke around us. He understands our secrets. He understands how hard forgiving can be. He felt our bitterness. His ultimate example is painstakingly clear. In the final chapter of his earth life, as recorded in Luke 22–23, we read how he met the challenge of the celestial laws of forgiveness. He suffered in agony greater in the Garden of Gethsemane than any of us could endure. There he not only took upon himself the sins of the world but every secret: our afflictions, temptations, infirmities, and sicknesses. Then he was betrayed, arrested, beaten, and mocked. Following a trial and the release of Barabbas, the nails were driven into his hands, feet, and wrists and he was hung on a cross.

Was it fair? Had he done anything to warrant their insane behavior? It was the greatest mockery of justice to the only one free of sin who has lived on the earth. And moreover, as Spencer W. Kimball, then a member of the Quorum of the Twelve Apostles, said, "Remember that we must forgive even if our offender did not repent and ask forgiveness. . . . The Lord Jesus also gave to us the lesson. Before they asked forgiveness, before they repented, while they were still in their murderous passion, he found it in his heart to forgive them and to ask his Father to '. . . forgive them; for they know not what they do.' (Luke 23:34.) He did not wait till his crucifiers . . . should have a change of heart, but forgave them while they were yet covered with his life's blood." (In Conference Report, October 1949, p. 132.)

Yes, the Savior understands our pain. And with his help and his grace, we can always forgive.

I believe, my brethren and sisters, that there is a need in the world for emphasis to be given to a great principle of which the Lord has spoken many times and which his apostles, old and modern, have advocated. That is the need of our being more charitable, and I assume that need exists among us. I know that it exists with me. . . .

I have in mind the charity that impels us to be sympathetic, compassionate, and merciful, not only in times of sickness and affliction and distress, but also in times of weakness or error on the part of others.

. . . The more perfect one becomes, the less he is inclined to speak of the imperfections of others.

—*ElRay L. Christiansen*

10
The Pure Love of Christ

THE SCRIPTURES TELL US THAT "charity is the pure love of Christ" (Moroni 7:47). Charity is of such importance that the Book of Mormon begins and ends with great charitable examples. Nephi was a righteous young man whose life was sometimes made miserable by two older brothers, Laman and Lemuel. They apparently liked to rough him up when he made them angry. Once, when returning to the wilderness after enlisting Ishmael and his family to go with them, one of those emotional boiling points occurred. Laman, Lemuel, and four members of Ishmael's family decided to return to Jerusalem, where they had wealth, friends, and security. Why would they want to dwell in the wilderness? When Nephi tried to stop them, they bound him and tried to kill him.

Reading about a distant Book of Mormon prophet, it's easy for us to think, *Laman and Lemuel sure were mean to Nephi.* But put yourself in his place. How would you react if some of your brothers or sisters tied you up and tried to kill you?

Here is how Nephi charitably handled the situation: "And it came to pass that I did frankly forgive them all that they had done" (1 Nephi 7:21).

Few people can read the testimony of Moroni without weeping for his great losses. His life and the life of his father, Mormon, stand as a witness to us that individuals can be righteous and stand stead-fast despite the total wickedness around them. In Mormon 7 we read: "Behold I, Moroni, do finish the record of my father, Mormon . . . for I am alone. My father hath been slain in battle, and all my kinsfolk, and I have not friends nor whither to go; and how long the Lord will suffer that I may live I know not." (Mormon 8:1, 5.)

Moroni had lost everyone. The remainder of his life, which re-markably consisted of thirty-six years of solitude, hiding, and writing and protecting the records, could have been full of hatred for the wicked Lamanites. After all, look what they had done to his friends, his family, and the whole Nephite nation. In the final battle of Cu-morah, over 230,000 Nephites were slain. And yet, in perhaps one of the greatest examples of charity, he says, "But I write a few more things, that perhaps they may be of worth unto *my brethren, the Lamanites,* in some future day, according to the will of the Lord" (Moroni 1:4; emphasis added).

That is charity. That is the pure love of Christ.

Do you feel like you're there yet? In life, we have sprinkles of pure charity. But how will we ever arrive at the pure-love-of-Christ level? Moroni 7:48 tells us the way: "Wherefore, my beloved brethren, pray unto the Father with all the energy of heart, that ye may be filled with this love, which he hath bestowed upon all who are true followers of his Son, Jesus Christ; that ye may become the sons of God; that when he shall appear we shall be like him, for we shall see him as he is; that we may have this hope; that we may be purified even as he is pure. Amen."

If we want to be purified even as he is pure, we must pray to our Father in Heaven with all of the energy of our heart that he will lead us to do the things that will make us pure. With all of the energy of our heart can't be one of those "Now I lay me down to sleep" prayers. It's not one of those prayers that we have when we are tired and hop into bed having forgotten to say our prayers, and when we remember we close our eyes in bed and doze off before we finish. It's a prayer given when we have blocked out some special prayer time. We kneel, visualize whom we're speaking to, even speak aloud, and then take time to ponder and listen. That kind of a prayer is carried with us throughout the day. A daily habit of that kind of prayer can change our lives.

The Spirit can teach us all day if we are where we are supposed to be, such as attending our meetings and visiting those the Spirit prompts us to visit. He will teach us through others, as we read, and as we listen to the Spirit. Because we have been told that "out of small things proceedeth that which is great" (D&C 64:33), we can begin with little changes, knowing they will lead us to become like him.

In fact, it's the little things that point out our characters and give us a starting point. One small, humorous example will teach this point. Have you ever seen an empty toilet-paper roll? It may have small shreds of paper on it, but certainly not enough to help the next user of the roll. Whom was the person just before you thinking about?

In the Book of Mormon, Mosiah tells about King Noah, who ruled in wickedness. His main focus was outlined in Mosiah 11:2: "For behold, he did not keep the commandments of God, but he did *walk after the desires of his own heart*" (emphasis added). In other words, King Noah was selfish. He wasted his days in laziness, idolatry, and whoredoms and levied a heavy tax of one-fifth of all his people possessed. His people labored "exceedingly to support iniquity" (Mosiah 11:6).

Charity or selfishness? Which one do we want to fill our time with? Elder Marvin J. Ashton of the Quorum of the Twelve Apostles said, "Real charity is not something you give away; it is something that you acquire and make a part of yourself" ("The Tongue Can Be a Sharp Sword," *Ensign*, May 1992, p. 19). Make it part of you by remembering the small things. Do you make sure your garbage hits the intended container, and if it doesn't do you shrug your shoulders and leave it on the floor? Whose desires are you thinking about? If you need a cup and the only cups are in the just-finished dishwasher, will you be the one to put the dishes back into the cupboard? If you need to empty the garbage in the kitchen, and when you take it out the garbage can is still in the street, and the garbagemen have already come, will you be the one to take the big can off the street? Try being hyperaware of those little things for a week. It's an enlightening experience.

Charity can then be bumped up a level. Look for little things to do that take a little more energy and time. In a letter to the editor of a newspaper, Irene Staples told of a wonderful example of this level of charity:

> One evening I was hosting a special guest from New York City. We were on our beautiful Temple Square, admiring the Seagull Monument. As we turned to go, four teenagers approached us. I immediately felt the [in]security of my gentleman guest, when one of the group stepped forward and said, "Lady, we would like to present you with this rose to make you happy, and hope that you will have a nice evening."
>
> There clutched in his hand was a beautiful, long-stemmed American Beauty red rose, with a spray of fern, artistically wrapped in cellophane.
>
> "We bought this rose to give to someone, and when we saw you, we thought you were the one."
>
> As they turned to leave, I quickly got their names, expressing my most profound appreciation and admiration for their thoughtfulness and kindness to me, which was so unusual, and how I was quite overwhelmed to think that four teenagers would have the desire for such a gracious act, and that no one would appreciate it more than I would, a little grandmother, as I gave each one a big hug. (As quoted in Robert L. Backman, " 'As I Have Loved You,' " *Ensign*, November 1985, p. 14.)

It cost the teenagers money for a rose and some time. The mind-set is to simply think of someone besides yourself. Sometimes we find we are so busy living our lives that we don't take time to be charitable. This attitude can have tragic consequences, as told in an editorial comment given on KSL radio in Salt Lake City, Utah:

> Recently, two youngsters were killed while trying to cross busy Redwood Road on a tricycle during the afternoon rush hour. They were four and five years old.
>
> Apparently, the boys made it most of the way across the high-way before they were hit.
>
> Many questions about the incident come to mind. Of course, nothing can change the outcome. But your answer to one question might change the outcome for similar incidents in the future. What would you have done if you had been driving home on Redwood Road that evening?
>
> If you should see two tots struggling to cross a busy highway, what would you do?
>
> Perhaps as many as one hundred drivers passed those two youngsters. It seems logical that some may even have stopped to allow the two boys passage. Surely, someone could have gotten out of his or her car to escort the boys safely across the highway.
>
> The incident is symbolic of the self-centered world in which so many of us operate—always in a hurry, always thinking someone else will take care of the problem, always reluctant to take time out for someone else.
>
> It isn't that we don't care about others. We do care. We're very generous when it's convenient. But too often concern does not be-come action. (Editorial Comment, KSL Radio-TV, Salt Lake City, Utah, November 16, 1992. Used by permission.)

As we seek to become like our Savior, our concern has to be-come action. We need to take the time for the things that matter most. Sometimes the receiver of our charity is an easy target, like the grandmother on Temple Square. But what about someone who is different and isn't liked as well as others. Elder Ashton gave us some practical steps that will move us to that level of charity: "Perhaps the greatest charity comes when we are kind to each other, when we don't judge or categorize someone else, when we simply give each other the benefit of the doubt or remain quiet. Charity is accepting someone's differences, weaknesses, and shortcomings; having patience with someone who has let us down; or resisting the impulse to become offended when someone doesn't handle something the way we might have hoped. Charity is refusing to take advantage of another's weakness and being willing to forgive someone who has hurt us. Charity is expecting the best of each other." ("The Tongue Can Be a Sharp Sword," p. 19.)

Accepting someone's differences can be particularly tough in high school. Being the same as everyone else has always been a top priority. Those who appear different are ridiculed as others emotionally mash them trying to elevate themselves.

But, as Elder Ashton so nicely put it, "What is the antidote for this bashing that hurts feelings, demeans others, destroys relationships, and harms self-esteem? Bashing should be replaced with charity." ("The Tongue Can Be a Sharp Sword," p. 18.)

A wonderful story illustrating this point was told by Elder Robert L. Backman of the Seventy:

> Fern attended high school in a small town. She was one of those nice but unnoticed girls who don't become much but a face on a yearbook page and a name on the rolls. Her family was poor, and they lived out of town. She was not part of the "in crowd," and the only time her name came up in a conversation of other students was in that mocking, sarcastic way that seems funny when you are young, insecure, and need to ridicule someone else to take the pressure off yourself. Her name became synonymous with anything

dumb or out of style. If a thing was unacceptable or ridiculous, the students called it "Ferny."

Young people can be so cruel.

It was an annual tradition in the school to recognize the student who showed the most school spirit and support for the athletic teams. When the assembly came to honor that student, as expected, they called out the name of one of the more popular girls in the school. She bounced up the aisle smiling and waving to all her friends. But then a miracle happened. As she took the stage, she said, "I can't accept this award. Yes, I have loved the teams and cheered for them at every game. But Fern has come to every game, too. I came in a nice, warm car surrounded by my happy friends. She came alone and walked all the way—two and a half miles—sometimes in the rain or snow. She had to sit by herself, but I don't know anyone who cheered with as much spirit as Fern. I would like to nominate her for the most enthusiastic student in the school."

Fern was escorted to the stage to a spontaneous standing ovation from her fellow students.

Youth can be so kind.

Fern is a mature woman today, her hair streaked with gray. Many things have happened to shape her life, but nothing more important than that outburst of acceptance and appreciation from her peers on that memorable day.

And there are mature men and women today who can't remember how many games their teams won or lost that year, but who have never forgotten the warm feeling they had when they stood up and cheered for Fern and welcomed her into their friendship and society. (" 'As I Have Loved You,' " p. 12.)

Elder Ashton also said: "None of us need one more person bashing or pointing out where we have failed or fallen short. Most of us are already well aware of the areas in which we are weak. What each of us does need is family, friends, employers, and brothers and sisters who support us, who have the patience to teach us, who believe in us, and who believe we're trying to do the best we can, in spite of our weaknesses. What ever happened to giving each other the benefit of the doubt? What ever happened to hoping that another person would succeed or achieve? What ever happened to rooting for each other?" ("The Tongue Can Be a Sharp Sword," p. 19.)

Rooting for everyone, even those who have problems, is a special form of charity. When someone is giving a talk and is struggling with it, do we inwardly critique them or do we take the opportunity to pray for their success and try to let the spirit of what they are trying to say teach us? The Spirit can teach us all things. Besides moving us toward our goal of obtaining the pure love of Christ, being charitable keeps us from moving in the wrong direction.

Elder Ashton also said: "If the adversary can influence us to pick on each other, to find fault, bash, and undermine, to judge or humiliate or taunt, half his battle is won. Why? Because though this sort of conduct may not equate with succumbing to grievous sin, it nevertheless neutralizes us spiritually. The Spirit of the Lord cannot dwell where there is bickering, judging, contention, or any kind of bashing." ("The Tongue Can Be a Sharp Sword," p. 20.)

Everyone who is a member of the Church has been given a gift by the Spirit of God. Some are given a testimony to know that Jesus Christ is the Son of God. Some are given the gift of wisdom; some can discern spirits. We each have at least one gift. Many have multiple gifts. We are told that we should seek earnestly for these gifts, that we should ask our Father in Heaven for specific gifts to benefit others (see D&C 46:8). The gift of charity is the greatest gift we can be given. Feel the strength of this gift in the following story:

Ronny was not just shy; he was downright backward. As a 17-year-old high school senior, Ronny had never really had a close friend or done anything that included other people. He was famous for his shyness. He never said anything to anybody, not even a teacher. One look at him told you a great deal of the story—inferiority complex. He slumped over as if to hide his face and seemed to be always looking at his feet. He always sat in the back of the class and would never participate. . . .

It was because of Ronny's shyness that I was so astonished when he started coming to my Sunday School class. . . .

His attendance in my class was the result of the personal efforts of a classmember, Brandon Craig, who had recently befriended Ronny. Boy, if there had ever been a mismatch, this was it. Brandon was "Mr. Social." A good head taller than Ronny, he was undisputedly the number one star of our high school athletics program. Brandon was involved in everything and successful at everything. . . . He was just a neat kid.

Well, Brandon took to little Ronny like glue. Class was obviously painful for Ronny, but Brandon protected him like the king's guard. I played a low profile—no questions, just a quick smile and once a pat on the back. Time seemed to be helping, but I often wondered if Brandon and company (the rest of the class certainly played it right) would ever be able to break the ice. That's why I was so shocked when Brian, the class president, stood before our Sunday School class one Sunday afternoon and boldly announced that Ronny would offer the opening prayer.

There was a moment of hesitation; then Ronny slowly came to his feet. Still looking at his shoes, he walked to the front of the room. He folded his arms (his head was already bowed). The class was frozen solid. I thought to myself, "If he does it, we'll all be translated."

Then almost at a whisper I heard, "Our Father in Heaven, thank you for our Sunday School class." Then silence—long, loud silence! I could feel poor Ronny suffering. Then came a few sniffles and a muffled sob.

"Oh, no," I thought, "I should be up front where I can help or something."

I hurt for him; we all did. I opened an eye and looked up to make my way to Ronny. But Brandon beat me to it. With an eye still open I watched six-foot-four Brandon put his arm around his friend, bend down and put his chin on Ronny's shoulder, then whisper the words of a short, sweet prayer. Ronny struggled for composure, then repeated the prayer.

But when the prayer was over, Ronny kept his head bowed and added: "Thank you for Brandon, amen." He then turned and looked up at his big buddy and said clear enough for all to hear, "I love you, Brandon."

Brandon, who still had his arm around him, responded, "I love you too, Ronny. And that was fun."

And it was, for all of us. (D. Brent Collette, "Ronny's Buddy," *New Era*, May 1983, p. 18.)

Now let's consider another level of charity that would be difficult for all of us. It's the charity that is given when circumstances make it severely trying to give to others. Brother LeRoy Skidmore of the Tooele Sixth Ward showed us all how to die with the crown of charity. He and his wife, Vilo, were stalwarts of the ward. They weren't showy but always quietly did wonderful things. Brother Skidmore contracted cancer and endured many painful months of treatment and sickness. Because he was such a fine man, many wondered, "Why him?" Because of the strength of his testimony, we never heard complaint or questioning. Even in his weakened condition, he wrote many letters commending or encouraging those who had participated in any Church meeting or activity. Those letters are treasures to us and to our children. He bore a powerful testimony of his blessings and the love of the Lord. When he could no longer get off his couch, he continued calling for home-teaching reports. Those who visited him came away marveling at his ability to cheerfully divert their attention from his illness to his interest in their family's activities. We went to his home and always came away buoyed by his and his wife's accepting and loving attitudes. That's an upper-division type of charity.

Another example of this level of charity was told by Scott Gardiner, who had been a police officer in Salt Lake City for seventeen years:

> I've made thousands of arrests for traffic violations. Most arrests are so strikingly similar that they blend together with few distinguishing differences.
>
> But one arrest—on a cold, dark wintry night in 1993—not only enriched my life, but taught me that judging people by their appearance is a poor barometer of the quality of their souls.
>
> The arrest began like so many others. A driver of a 1960s model pickup truck seemed to show little regard for traffic safety. I hit the lights on my motorcycle and pulled him over.
>
> He was about 35 years old. His face was grimy and his hair wind-blown, and considering the rusted patches of his truck and his shabby clothing, he appeared very poor. His wife sat beside him in the seat, looking very much his equal.
>
> I wondered how people could live in such desperate circumstances. "Didn't they have any self-respect? Where was their ambition to improve their condition?" I thought to myself.
>
> After going through the routine of the arrest and handcuffing him, I noticed how the bed of his pickup truck was loaded with old, tattered clothing which was covered with soot.
>
> I asked him where he got the clothing. Looking down, as if ashamed, he said that he and his wife regularly went to the viaducts on the western side of the city where the homeless huddle in large groups to warm themselves around fires built in 100-gallon drums.
>
> He described how the fires blacken the transients' clothing and faces with soot. And even though he and his wife didn't have much more themselves, they would gather the sooty clothing, take it to their residence where they would wash and return the clothing the next day.
>
> I was spiritually stunned. Here were two people of meager

means demonstrating love for their fellowmen. Here was charity where I didn't expect it.

In the next days, I tried to think of someone I knew who would leave the comforts of their home and rub shoulders with the unwashed masses. But I could think of no one.

I found new meaning in the Savior's admonition. "Thou shalt love thy neighbor as thyself."

I also found new condemnation. If they—who had so few possessions—could give so willingly, how much more would be required of me—who comparatively has so much.

These two had no material wealth, but they were sharing what little they had. ("More to a person than haggard appearance," *Church News*, November 9, 1996, p. 11. Reprinted from *LDS Church News* with permission.)

That's the pure love of Christ. Can we attain it? Yes, with his help. Remember, everyone has secrets. Pray to Heavenly Father to know how best to help. He knows all of their secrets, and through listening to the whisperings of the still, small voice, we will be blessed with understanding and react with charity.

Index